Published and distributed by Lulu.c
ISBN: 978-1-291-44850-4

© Rocky Mason. All rights reserved.

No part of this book may be reproduced, stored in a retrieval system or transmitted by any means without the written permission of the author.

All images in this book are copyright of Rocky Mason or have received the appropriate clearance..

Any views expressed in the book are solely those of the author and does not necessarily reflect the views of the publisher or the book designer who disclaim any responsibility for them

Book layout and front cover produced by Irnwurks Media
http://www.irnwurksmedia.eu

Butlins in its Prime
(Those Golden Years)

By

Rocky Mason

Contents

Chapter One	Arrival on Fantasy Island
Chapter Two	Falling in love with Butlins
Chapter Three	I want to be a G.D Redcoat
Chapter Four	I want to be an entertainer
Chapter Five	Filey in The cold, cold winter
Chapter Six	Into my second season
Chapter Seven	Boxing exhibitions
Chapter Eight	Winter at Brighton
Chapter Nine	Charlie Paints a Picture
Chapter Ten	Winter at Margate
Chapter Eleven	Back to dear old Filey
Chapter Twelve	Minehead's opening season
Chapter Thirteen	Margate and I meet Marty
Chapter Fourteen	"Croeso Y Cymru"
Chapter Fifteen	Hotels for the Winter
Chapter Sixteen	Bognor Regis
Chapter Seventeen	Skegness
Chapter Eighteen	Sir Billy goes to Jersey
Chapter Nineteen	I become a proud father
Chapter Twenty	We buy High Lodge
Chapter Twenty One	Butlins feel the pinch
Chapter Twenty Two	Back to beloved Filey

I dedicate this book, with great love,
to my three girls.

Marty, Sam and Ellie.

About The Author

Rocky joined Butlins Filey in 1957 as a Redcoat Boxing Instructor. He later asked to become a General Duty Redcoat to give him more opportunity to mix with the guests.

He became permanent staff in 1958 and went to the Butlin Ocean Hotel, Brighton, for the winter. The following year he became Chief Redcoat and had his own late night show 'Rendezvous With Rocky'. In 1962 he joined the management team as Deputy Entertainment Manager at the opening of the new camp at Minehead. In the winter he became manager of the Margate group of hotels, he also became the company's Senior Compere, presenting the televised Grand Finals of the major competitions.

After two seasons as Deputy Entertainment Manager at Pwllheli he became Entertainment Manager at Bognor, transferring to Skegness half way through the season, where in 1966 he introduced Midnight Cabaret. He remained at Skegness until 1970 when he was moved to Pwllheli camp in North Wales.

His next few years were spent moving between the hotels in the winter and camps in the summer, remaining at Pwllheli until 1974 when he returned to Filey as Leisure & Amenities Controller. Heading up every department except, catering accommodation and children's nursery. Rocky remained at Filey until the closure of the camp in 1983.

He then moved to Leisure Holidays, a subsidiary of Butlins and ran the entertainment in Cornwall.

Rocky knew the Butlin family well and was proud to be asked to be an usher at Sir Billy's memorial service at St Martin's-in-the-Field London.

He remained in contact with Bobby long after they had both retired from the company and Bobby, who shunned publicity, gave Rocky information for the inclusion of his early life in 'Gumshield to Greasepaint', one of Rocky's earlier works. Some of that rare material is included here.

Thank You

The author would like to express his grateful thanks to his wife Marty for keeping him fed and watered and for her patience and understanding during the many months spent penning these pages.

Thanks also to Frank McGroarty of Irnwurks Media for the design and layout of this entire book. Also for preparing the photographs for print.

FOREWORD

Tony Peers: Comedian, Actor, Theatre Producer also Freeman of Scarborough and the City of London.

This is a book about a man I admire, written by a man I admire, about a philosophy and a way of life I admire, so being asked to write the Foreword for this book involved me in a labour of love.

Billy Butlin created more than holiday camps when he opened his first one at Skegness in 1936. He created a philosophy and a way of life for holidaymakers and staff alike. In a stroke of genius he invented the legendary Redcoat whose role was to mix and mingle with and entertain the guests. Inevitably, in building an empire the size of Butlins, myths and legends are created of what supposedly went on at various times. This book tells the definitive story of Butlins as it really was, separating the myths from the true facts and gives an affectionate look back at a golden era of Billy Butlins dream.

Written by Rocky Mason a legendary Butlins Entertainment Manager and close confidante of Sir Billy who 'was there'. If anyone could be described as the archetypal Redcoat made good then it is Rocky Mason, from his early days as a Redcoat to his ascension to the dizzy heights of Leisure and Amenities Controller of Butlins biggest camp at Filey. Rocky was a Redcoat, Boxing Instructor, Chief Redcoat, Entertainment Manager, Show Producer and Butlins Senior Compere and Rocky could only be described as larger than life.

Rocky has a million stories about Butlins, some involving himself and some others. He now draws back the curtain and shows us the real Butlins - "Butlins in its Prime".

Tony Peers

Introduction: Rocky Mason

There have been many books written about Butlins and no doubt there will be many more, and my only excuse for adding one more to the list is that I want to destroy the myths. In the many books written about Billy Butlin the writers have, in an effort to establish the kindly man image, flattered and embellished him. As a result all the books effectively tell his story but give little insight into Billy Butlin the man, the enigma who was a quiet-spoken warm-hearted character with a wicked sense of humour-and yet also a shrewd businessman, capable of being totally ruthless. A great many myths surround Sir Billy, and one of the most repeated is of how he started his holiday camps after spending a rainy holiday on Barry Island in South Wales. It is said his boarding house landlady insisted on the guests leaving the premises after breakfast and not returning until dinner in the evening. It rained incessantly throughout his holiday and Billy felt sorry for himself, they say, but even sorrier for the families with young children as they trudged around wet and bedraggled, or forlornly filled in time in amusement arcades until they could return to their boarding houses. That, like so many other stories about the great man is a complete fantasy and the real reason is disclosed in this book. That and many other falsehoods are dispelled within these pages.

He didn't suffer fools lightly and was completely without humbug or pretension, he had a quiet and sometimes wicked sense of humour and I have tried to illustrate this. His humour was displayed when he said *"For public addresses I have only two speeches - one short and one long, The short one is 'thank you', and the long one is 'thank you very much.'"*

The passing of time is remorseless and the years relentlessly come and go and as the years slip by so do memories of times past and therefore some kind of factual record must be left because, painful as it is, one day there will be nobody left to remember.

If you were a camper or knew Butlins only as a visitor this collection of anecdotes will give you an indication of some of the things that went on behind the scenes. If you were a Redcoat or former member of staff you will perhaps relive your memories through a different pair of eyes. Whatever, I'm sure you will enjoy.

Chapter One

I WILL NEVER FORGET, NOR WOULD I EVER WANT TO FORGET, the feeling of joy as I stepped through the gates of Butlins, Filey, it was May 1957 and little did I realise then that it would lead to a career lasting 30 years. It was almost like stepping into wonderland and, after walking for a hundred yards or so, I had to stop and stand in amazement just looking round and trying to take everything in. I was being bathed in pleasant music coming from speakers suspended from high buildings and concealed in trees. I could hear laughter and other sounds of happiness from people surrounding the large blue and white swimming pool. There was cheerful music and singing coming from one building, laughter and applause from another. I was enthralled by the sight of exotic flowers in every tree and shrub - I would later learn that the blooms were plastic but it mattered not a bit. I was awed by the coloured lanterns hanging over every road. I had started to walk again but had to stop and stare in wonder at the sheer beauty of a fountain in the boating lake; it was shimmering and dancing high into the sky. My eyes were drawn to the cries of joy and laughter of children actually splashing and playing in more fountains at each end of the pool. I saw people, with happy faces, rowing colourful boats on a beautiful shrub lined lake.

I was 26 years old, in the prime of my life, as handsome as I was ever going to be, and beautiful girls were coming at me round ever corner. I started to notice young men and women in red blazers and white skirts or trousers, all of them smiling or laughing, calling out to people and chatting or waving. They would be the people I had come to join; they were the famous Butlin Redcoats. So this was it then! The Butlins my friends had told me about and now I was seeing it for myself on this my very first visit. I couldn't make up my mind, had I somehow stepped into Wonderland, or was it Paradise or indeed Fantasy Island?

After checking into the entertainment office, where I met the chief Redcoat Johnny O'Mahoney, who told me to pronounce his name 'O'Marney'. I was given a clothing issue form and told to collect my uniform from the clothing store. I was later told that Johnny was the brother of Irish comedian Dave O'Mahoney, who would change his name to Dave Allen and become one of the biggest names on television. I was also given a list called "Standing Instructions to Redcoats" and a copy of the entertainment programme which listed the various activities and events taking place around the camp. I was told the full Redcoat induction meeting would take place at 9.0'clock the following morning.

After drawing my uniform and settling into my chalet, the rest of the day was mine to explore at my leisure. I was surprised at the smallness of the chalet, it was very basic to say the least and roughly 10 feet square, and it contained a double bunk-bed, which was one small single bed on top of another, so I gathered I would be sharing. It also contained a small wardrobe with a curtain instead of a door. There was a four drawer chest and I packed my things into the two top drawers and, by putting my robe under the pillows, I reserved the bottom bunk.

There was no toilet or shower and I would later discover these were in blocks further down the chalet line. I noticed in the small wash basin there was just one tap and it was marked "cold", hot water could be obtained from taps outside the toilet blocks and each chalet had a jug for this purpose.

Later, when I started to explore I was spellbound by everything I saw, enormous ballrooms, theatres and bars and all of them decorated in a particular theme. The Viennese Ballroom really was 'out of this world' there was a huge tree 'growing' out of the centre of the floor and reaching to the ceiling. A closer inspection established it was plastic but very life-like. There was a balcony where people could sit and watch the dancing. I made an effort to count the number of seats but got confused so gave a calculated guess of around 2,000.

There was a grand piano on the stage covered in mirror glass, the stage had red and gold curtains and the white back drop was covered in twinkling lights. The roof girders were boxed in with sham bamboo boxes and had colourful plastic flowers and vines trailing from every box, making the ceiling look, for all the world, like a living-growing garden. The dance floor was highly polished and gave off a strong smell of lavender.

One of the exits from the Viennese took me into the French Bar, with a sign on the door proclaiming it to be "The Longest Bar In The World". There was a mighty Wurlitzer organ framed behind glass and a sign announcing it as the largest organ in the world. Colourful murals on the walls depicted Paris scenes with the Eiffel Tower, Arc de Triumph and scores of Can-Can dancers. A closer look told me that the paintings had been done by the famous Helen McKay RA.

All the doors to the bar were open and I saw there was a series of shutters to protect the stock, yet another door took me out into the enormous amusement park where there was a giant big wheel, dodgems, lots of swings and slides a high rollercoaster ride called "The Wild Mouse". The centrepiece was a gigantic ride called "The Golden Galloping Horses" with a sign on it promising 'Our True Intent Is All For Your Delight'. Music from yet another Titanic organ was blaring out around the park and above this could be heard the excited screams of girls and young children.

I left the fairground to visit the outdoor swimming pool, painted in a beautiful shade of blue which, I would soon discover, was Billy Butlins favourite colour and was in fact called 'Butlin Blue'. There was a sign on the diving board to inform people that the length was 'Olympic' size but as the pool was much wider it made it the 'Largest Pool In Europe'. I was quickly learning that my new boss Billy Butlin didn't do things by half measure! There were six tennis courts and all of them in use, the crazy golf and putting greens were also busy and being enjoyed by happy people and the playing fields just stretched for miles. All the camp roads were bordered by the most beautiful rose gardens and rockeries. I would later be informed that the camp was 400 acres, the largest holiday camp in the world and regarded by Billy Butlin as 'The flagship of the fleet'. Entering the Playhouse Theatre, housing the Forbes Russell Repertory Company, was like stepping into the past. It had a rainbow shaped, proscenium arch painted in glittering gold. The walls of the theatre were papered in black and red flock paper. The stage curtains were in a rich red velvet. It was almost a replica of the Leeds Palace Of Varieties, and it would seat an audience of around 600.

The Empire Theatre, which was used for band shows, junior and senior talent contests, games shows, late night shows and films, was just as attractive but had a modern theme and would seat over a thousand. The Gaiety Theatre presenting the resident revue shows, Sunday Variety and Redcoat Show was larger still and had a revolving stage. I noticed that in all the venues, although not actually open and in use, there was pleasant background music playing which seemed to enhance the building and make it feel welcoming. I would later be told the music was relayed from Radio Butlin, the camps own radio station.

I was delighted to find rows and rows of chalets and all of them divided into 'camps' and, like the other buildings, painted in a wonderful array of colours. It was all so big it was awesome, breathtaking, and I found myself constantly taking my chalet key from my pocket to glance at it - B27 Blue camp and I was making a determined effort not to get lost.

When I made my way back to my chalet to wash and change for the evening I as in a very happy frame of mind. During my tour I had made a remarkable discovery, there was no admission charge for entry into any of the theatres; no fee was to be paid for any of the facilities I had seen. On the amusement park all the rides had been free, and there was no charge for anything from crazy golf to swimming and boating. Looking around the large games rooms I had seen there was nothing to be paid for table tennis, billiards, snooker and darts. It was simply a matter of handing over your chalet key as a deposit for the equipment. What a joy for parents! Especially those with two or three children. Once they had paid their initial tariff there was nothing else to pay and the kids could go on everything, all day and every day, with dad never once having to put his hand in his pocket.

Johnny had told me to take my evening meal in Gloucester dining hall and that a bluecoat supervisor would find me a seat. I was to learn that each enormous dining room had a name and the meals came in two sittings. Each sitting was called a 'House' and there was Kent, Gloucester, York, Edinburgh Windsor and Connaught. Each house had a house captain and a team of Redcoats.

There were wooden steps leading up to the house captain's rostrum and microphone. This was where the house captain would make a 'spiel' at every meal, his spiel would be mainly jocular *"This is your handsome House Captain Dusty speaking. Today we are going to enjoy 80 degrees of glorious sunshine!! …..40 in the morning and 40 in the afternoon!"*

On the wall above the rostrum was the champagne spinner, which looked like an enormous clock containing all the rows and table numbers in the room. At every evening meal the house captain would spin for a bottle of champagne and a team of Redcoats would line up to march, clapping and cheering, around the room, to present the champagne to the lucky winners. In the region of two thousand campers would be applauding in unison and so the noise was pretty awesome. Woe betide the poor unfortunate waitress who dropped a plate, as this hapless girl would be almost cheered out of the room. You could, of course, always depend on the cheering being led by your 'Friends Philosophers and Guides' The good old Redcoats!

During the meal I noticed the plates of food were kept warm in heated Jackson's, which were enormous metal cabinets on wheels and plugged into electric sockets around the walls. I was pleasantly surprised at the standard of the food and thought it was similar to food I had eaten during my military National Service, but marginally better and I really enjoyed the meal.

I felt quite excited as I set out to explore the evening's activities that I had studied in the programme Johnny had given me. I didn't sit through an entire show but did visit all the theatres. The first was the delightful Playhouse Theatre, where I saw the Forbes Russell Players were presenting the first house of "Bell, Book and Candle", it had been written a few years before in 1950 and the original had starred Rex Harrison and his then wife Lilli Palmer. I had seen in the programme that most of the shows were presented in two performances and, with around 10,000 campers to entertain, I could quite understand the need for that, despite the wide variety of other entertainment taking place at the same time. The variety show in the Gaiety Theatre was playing to a capacity audience and I counted 14 musicians in the orchestra pit. I was interested to see that the Redcoats were like ushers, manning the doors and chatting to people as they entered and I quickly discovered that a beaming smile was an important piece of Redcoat equipment. The Empire Theatre was closed but a billboard announced that there would be a family film show starting at 8.00pm. As I did the rounds I introduced myself, where possible, to Redcoats and I found them all friendly and helpful. I discovered the host in the large Viennese Ballroom was Teddy Foster, fronting a 22 piece orchestra which included a male and female vocalist.

The male singer was Dean Raymond, who had enjoyed modest success with a couple of singles which I recalled hearing on the late night Radio Luxembourg. The female was Julie Rolls; I listened to a few of her numbers and decided she was an excellent vocalist. We would become friends over the next few years until Julie eventually left to marry Teddy and tour the American bases in Germany where Julie was seen by Johnny Franz at Philips Records, who signed her on a five year contract. She changed her name to Julie Rogers and her first release "It's Magic" was a huge success and introduced Julie to radio and TV. She then recorded "The Wedding" which soared to the top of The Hit Parade, selling fifteen million copies and, to coin a hackneyed phrase, a star was born. Of course neither of us could have imagined any of this then, not even in our wildest dreams. I most certainly didn't as I listened to the lovely voice of Julie Rolls on my first evening on Filey camp. The Viennese Ballroom was very busy and I had seen in the programme that a number of competitions and party dances were also featured there. The Regency Ballroom was less busy but the atmosphere suggested that this was the venue for serious dancing and I sat watching for a few moments as the men, in their shiny plastic dance shoes, led the ladies in waltzes and foxtrots. Dancing was to the Fred Percival fourteen piece dance band and they were excellent. There was a different form of entertainment in every bar, and every venue was packed with happy smiling campers. A team of Redcoats were keeping a large crowd happy playing bingo in the Welcome Inn. I was surprised to see they were paying for their tickets with cash, but the amounts they won in prizes were paid in Butlin vouchers. The Redcoat caller announced that they could be spent in the camp shops or as a deposit for a future holiday.

    I was somewhat surprised at this but I heard no rumbles of discontent. It didn't need Albert Einstein to work out that Butlins were in a win-win situation, making profit on the bingo and doubling it when the prize vouchers were spent in the camp shops. It was obvious that bingo was a fun event and, unlike some commercial halls I had seen, the caller and the Redcoats on the floor were all having fun and the campers were joining in and creating a lovely friendly atmosphere. I stood at the bar for a few moments amused by the banter and the calls… (Male voice)… *"Shake 'em up!!"* (Female caller)…*"I'll get big Janet to come over and shake you up in a minute!"*… *"All the fours it's droopy draws"* … *"McMillan's den, it's number ten"*

    In the Regency Bar, Johnny, the chief Redcoat, a Redcoat pianist and another on guitar were playing to a packed house and getting almost a standing ovation. Two Redcoat entertainers Miller & Merrick, who I later discovered were a husband and wife team, were in the French Bar, entertaining on piano accordion and drums. There was an excellent organ and drums duo playing for a Redcoat sing-song performing to a responsive crowd in the Gaiety Bar. I saw that every single member of the audience had laughter in their eyes and a smile on their face.

    I spent the last half hour in the Viennese Ballroom and watched as Teddy Foster played a session of 'smoochy' numbers to a packed dance floor. Julie sang and I saw that a few of the Redcoats were joining in the dancing. I recognised a number of Redcoats that I had seen in other venues earlier in the evening and so I presumed that when they had perhaps finished a theatre duty, or other detail, they then made their way to the ballroom to mix and mingle for the rest of the evening. The session was finished with a ritual that I imagined had been a Butlin tradition for quite a number of years. The girl Redcoat who I had seen calling bingo earlier, and had learned that she was known as 'Bingo Betty', came out on stage and made an announcement to the packed ballroom. It was to invite them to go onto the dance floor and line up in front of the stage. They were then asked to link arms with the persons standing each side of them. The girl had a warm personality and a good microphone technique. Her voice was as clear as a bell and it was obvious she was an experienced exponent on a microphone as she announced…

"The time has come to say goodnight, we hope you have had a wonderful day with us and I can promise you there will be another fabulous day tomorrow. I would ask you now to put your hands together in appreciation of the fantastic Teddy Foster and his orchestra." There was tremendous applause from an appreciative audience. *"And now everyone, let's hear it for the superb voices of two talented people Dean Raymond and Julie Rolls"* Another round of enthusiastic appreciation. *"And now, your appreciation please for your friends, philosophers and guides, your very own Filey Butlin Redcoats."*

The applause was unbelievable as the Redcoats came out in lines of boy-girl-boy-girl, from each side of the stage. The orchestra was playing an introduction in the background as the Redcoats started to slowly kick from side to side. I glanced at the front row of campers on the dance floor and they were doing the same. I sensed that they had all done it before and the ritual was a well practised routine. I recognised the tune as the orchestra began to play "Goodnight Sweetheart".

I listened to a few bars before I realised that the lyrics everyone was singing were different to the original song. Words I would come to know by heart over the next few weeks and the corny words of a song that would stay in my heart and mind for the rest of my life. The title had been changed, appropriately, to "Goodnight Campers". The girl redcoat, 'Bingo Betty' who was more than capable on a microphone concluded the evening by saying. *"As you go down the chalet lines please consider the elderly people and children who may be sleeping and help us to maintain peace and quiet in the lines late at night. Goodnight- God bless you all!"*

Goodnight Campers

Good-night, Campers, I can see you yawning,
Good-night, Campers, see you in the morning,
You must cheer up or you'll soon be dead,
For I've heard it said, Folks die in bed,
So we'll say good-night Campers,
Don't sleep in your braces;
Good-night Campers, put your teeth in Jeyes's
Drown your sorrow, bring the bottles back tomorrow
Good-night Campers, good-night.

I put myself to bed in my little chalet that night, feeling very pleased with my first day at Butlins and looking forward with great anticipation to what might lay ahead.

I was woken the next morning by angelic music coming from a speaker in the chalet and a young lady determined to tell me that her name was Marjory, and first sitting breakfast would be available at 8.15. I would soon learn that this was a regular morning routine and was known as Radio Butlins "Wakey-Wakey". I remembered that an induction meeting had been planned for 9.0'clock and so I got out of bed to make an early start. I would learn that the angelic music was the pianist Tolchard Evans playing 'The Singing Piano'.

I went to the Gloucester dining room again for breakfast and the same friendly bluecoat showed me to a seat. I had an excellent full English breakfast, but was a bit put out to be told that they didn't ever do toast. I reasoned that this was obviously due to the large numbers involved and I accepted that in peak weeks, with 12,000 people being catered for and each one wanting two rounds and that would make 24,000 rounds of toast. A pretty tall order by anyone's standards!! The house captain took up his microphone on the rostrum *"And this is Dusty, your handsome house captain, wishing a very good morning to the fantastic, glorious, most illustrious and mighty house of GLOUCESTER!!"* A thunderous cheer rattled the windows and the old lady opposite me spat her cornflakes all over my suit!

I had expected the induction meeting that started promptly on time, to be nothing more than a formal introduction to a new job and to last for maybe 30 minutes. In fact it went on for the best part of the day. Twelve of us were new Redcoats and there was one other young bloke with the title Trainee Assistant Manager. The meeting was opened by the entertainment manager Wilfred Orange, the man who had interviewed me for the job. After welcoming everyone, Mr Orange went on to describe in general, but somewhat briefly, the job of a Redcoat and what would be expected of us.

He then passed us over to Johnny, the chief Redcoat, who asked us to take out our copies of "Standing Instructions to Redcoats" and went over them piecemeal and in great detail, emphasising certain aspects such as the importance of always being on time and not keeping the customer waiting, being pleasant, always smiling and mixing and mingling. Johnny had a charming Irish brogue and, when speaking, his voice sounded rather cultured. I would later learn that Johnny had a BA and his father was the former owner/editor of the Dublin Times newspaper. He had a delightful Irish way of expressing himself. *"I intend to be telling you that good timekeeping is vital for Butlin Redcoats. Buses and trains run late but Redcoats are always on time!"*

After going through the "Standing Instructions" in great detail Johnny introduced Arthur Riding, the CSO. His title was chief sports organiser and he explained to us at length how to work out 'Bye's in competitions, after doing this he passed out useful copies of what we'd been shown. I always thought the position of CSO was important, His job was to organise the swimming gala, cricket matches, sports day, football, and all the other sports, competitions and events. I personally thought his job was distinctly in contrast to that of chief Redcoat, but within the next two seasons the position was phased out and the responsibility for his jobs was passed to the chief Redcoat.

I should have known that Butlins never did things by half! The talk by the CSO was followed by an hours lecture from the chief fire officer, who explained to us the importance of not allowing invalid carriages and push chairs to block gangways and exits in theatres and other venues. He explained the fire drill for various buildings and how to evacuate guests from these venues. He was followed by a nursery nurse who explained a few points about the baby crying system. The induction, at the end of the day, had been very detailed, informative and helpful. I came away from my first meeting realising that discipline was far stronger than I would have expected, but also understanding how essential that was.

Our induction was concluded with a very stringent tour of the camp.

This was conducted by an experienced male and female Redcoat who I gathered had a number of seasons under their belts. Again they were most efficient, insisting that each of us opened an unlocking bar on an emergency exit. They showed us light switches and microphone points and explained other things in the various venues that would be useful for us to know. It was on this tour of the camp that I first saw the facilities for boxing. We were taken to an enormous marquee and informed that it had originally been the Billy Smart's circus Big Top. There in the centre stood a full size ring, it was rather tatty and I got the impression that it would just about serve its purpose. The marquee had been pitched on level ground and there were no raised seating areas.

This would make it difficult for the audience to see the action in the ring. The changing rooms looked like a temporary arrangement of partition walls and there were no toilet or washing facilities. What a disappointment it was considering the opulence of everything in other venues and, it seemed, the boxing had been just tossed aside in a tent. I met up with my friend Harry later in the day, it was Harry who had recommended me for the job and it was a joy to see him again.

Chapter Two

THE SAD THING ABOUT NOT BEING IN THE FIRST INTAKE was that we were too late to be involved in any of the shows. There was the Redcoat Show, Old Time Music Hall, Western Night and Minstrel Show, all up and running and, as we had missed rehearsals, we couldn't be included. It didn't worry me at first but, as the weeks went by, I began to feel sorry that I had missed out as I didn't feel a complete Redcoat because the campers couldn't see me performing on stage and I felt as if a vital part of being a Redcoat was missing. I had a very small part in something called the "Who's Who Show" which took place on stage in the Gaiety Theatre on Saturday night when certain personalities were introduced to the campers on the first night of their holiday. There was the football coach, tennis and table tennis coach, the cricket coach, head lifeguard and a boxing instructor. There would also be a bluecoat supervisor, a photographer, a couple of waitresses and half a dozen Redcoats. On being introduced by the compere, and accompanied by a fanfare, you walked to the centre microphone, took your bow and then went upstage to stand on a rostrum until the rest had also been introduced. For me it was one of the highlights of the week and I loved it. I never ceased to be amazed at the volume of applause from 2,000 people and I revelled in it... *"Representing your team of boxing instructors - Yorkshires own*, the *champion Rocky Mason"* Just a slight wave of the hand brought thunderous applause and not a blow struck or a punch taken.

Butlins had a reputation for being a tremendous springboard for talent and had been described as the greatest nursery for budding 'wannabes' in the entire world. For anyone with a bit of talent it provided the perfect training ground and quite a number of former Redcoats had become famous. Des O'Connor, Bill Maynard and Clinton Ford had been Redcoats. Charlie Drake, like me, started as a boxing instructor. Not that having entertainment ability was a quality need to be a good Redcoat.

I discovered that the Redcoat who was playing guitar with Johnny and Ronnie was a Liverpool lad called Ronnie Hulme. He was a children's uncle who spent the day entertaining kids in the children's theatre. When he closed the theatre in the evening he liked nothing more than joining Johnny and Ronnie and making up a trio to sing in one of the bars. The young Liverpool performer was a singer song writer who loved to play and sing his own numbers. He was doing this in the Regency Bar one evening when Billy Butlin walked in accompanied by Wally Goodman, Wally was a former bandleader and was Colonel Brown's assistant. The audience were being very appreciative of Ronnie's songs and Billy asked Wally what it was that made a pop star. Wally explained that it was down to record sales. Billy then told Wally that if they got young Ronnie Hulme into a recording studio and made a record of a couple of his songs. By selling them as a holiday souvenir on all the camps he could quickly become a pop star and give Butlins some tremendous publicity. Billy reasoned that it shouldn't be difficult to achieve a million record sales, selling it on nine camps with a total average of around 75,000 guests each week. Ronnie Hulme was whisked away to be signed by Oriole records and to record two of his own numbers, 'We Will Make Love' and on the flip side 'Rainbow'.

Ronnie was accompanied by the Johnny Gregory orchestra and backed by the Mike Sammes singers and the end result was very good. His name was also changed to Russ Hamilton. This was long before the days of DVDs, and records in those days were 9" black plastic discs. "We Will Make Love" was played in the camp theatres before the shows, in the ballrooms during intervals. Over Radio Butlin into the lounges and round the swimming pool. The fact that it was a recording made by a Butlin Redcoat and could be purchased as a holiday souvenir was well plugged and record sales went through the roof. It also sold pretty well in 'the outside world' and Russ quickly achieved a million sales. In this country "We Will Make Love" replaced Elvis Presley's "All Shook Up" as number one in the Hit Parade and Russ received a golden disc.

Strange things were happening in the USA. American DJs started plugging 'Rainbow' which was the flip side, the American public loved the song and it became a number one on that side of the Ocean. Russ was invited to appear in the Golden Show on New York's Broadway, he topped the bill appearing above established stars like Harry Belafonte. For the first time in history, before or since, two golden discs were awarded for one record and I am sure that Russ would have been the first to agree that Butlins was a tremendous launching pad for anyone with a bit of talent.

The Sunday Meeting was held by the entertainment

manager and the chief Redcoat, and was attended by every Redcoat. I counted heads and was surprised to see there were sixty four. I had met most of them during the preceding week and knew a bit about each of them. There were six entertainers as such, the ones who had a 'Redcoat Entertainer' contract. Ronnie Hunter, the popular Geordie pianist. Miller & Merrick, and Robin & Terry Gee, were bar entertainers, Jeff Whitfield, brother of the famous Dave, a vocalist The remainder were general duty Redcoats, who were responsible for running the events in the entertainment programme. None of them entertainers as such, although most of them could knock out a few numbers on a sing-song and get away with doing a spot on Old Time Music Hall. Being a singer or entertainer was well down the list of what it took to make a first-class Redcoat. I saw the general duty Redcoats as the 'Coal Face Workers' the ones at the forefront, dealing with the campers on a day to day basis. They did the meeting and greeting, running the competitions and events throughout the day and mixing and mingling at every opportunity. They were trained to speak to everyone they passed or came across, and their motto was "You're never fully dressed without a smile".

They had the proud reputation of being the campers "Friends philosophers and guides" these were the Famous Butlin Redcoats, the ones on which the Legend of Redcoats was built. They came from an assortment of backgrounds and different walks of life; the lovely Patsy Bridle, always with a deep sun-tan, which complimented her almost white blond hair. Patsy had been a fashion and photographic model who had worked for Cherie Marshal and often appeared in Vogue magazine. Ronnie had been a club and cabaret pianist. Jeff Whitfield, like his brother, had worked cabaret and clubs, but in a lesser way. Terri, with the vivacious personality, had acquired it and honed it in a Manchester hairdressers. Johnny had been a school teacher and journalist. Betty Bingo had been a waitress in a restaurant and worked evenings in a bingo hall.

Gordon couldn't sing a note in tune and in every Opening and Finale of the Redcoat show was the only one in step. However, like most of the others, he was an excellent Redcoat and, when there was no one else around to chat to he would talk to the birds in the trees. Gerry Maxim was the 'posh' Redcoat, nicely spoken and always immaculate. Gerry's family were well-to-do and lived in Leeds. His mother would come to visit occasionally in the family's chauffeur driven car. I was told that Gerry received a weekly allowance to supplement his Redcoat wages and I believe that to be true. On his day off he would usually take one of the girls for tea at the Royal Hotel in Scarborough and they also went and returned by taxi. I liked Gerry and we became good friends. Harry, my fellow boxing instructor, had been ABA, Imperial Services and Golden Gloves lightweight boxing champion. His record showed over 200 fights and he'd only lost three.

We had met boxing in the services together. Harry had boxed in the army and I had boxed for the RAF. I was quite pleased with my own record of 87 fights and only losing eight. Sixty nine of my fights had been straight wins and 37 of them knockouts. I had boxed on a few occasions at the National Sporting club, the President of which was Colonel Basil Brown, also entertainment director of Butlins. Harry had become a Redcoat boxing instructor the previous year and had written telling me all about it and inviting me to join him. On his recommendation to Wilf Orange, I was interviewed and got the job. Ken Garden had been Welsh heavyweight champion but since giving up professionally, and enjoying a few pints, had blown up to 18 stones. The three of us were a good team and were working well together.

I was quickly learning a great deal about the Butlin Empire and its founder Billy Butlin although Warners and other camps had existed in one form or another long before Billy opened his first in 1936. It was Billy who turned holiday camps into a multi-million pound industry and an important aspect of the British way of life. Billy's full name was William Edmund Heygate Colbourne Butlin and he was born in Cape Town, South Africa on 29th September 1899. Billy's father, also called William, was the son of a clergyman. His mother, Bertha, was a member of the Hill family of Bristol who were well known as travelling showmen. They met when Bertha's family were working a country fair William visited, they met and shortly after they were married. Their marriage was not considered socially acceptable in his father's parish, in Gloucestershire, where they lived, and they emigrated to South Africa.

After Bertha's marriage to Billy's father failed, she returned to Bristol with young Billy, leaving him in the care of her sister Jessie, Bertha started travelling round the summer fairs. When he was twelve his mother remarried and emigrated to Canada leaving him in the care of his aunt for two years. When Bertha settled in Toronto she sent for Billy,. In 1915 Billy did a stint as a bugle boy in the Canadian army. The fact that he was under age was neither here nor there. He spent two years at the front, experiencing the horrors of trench warfare, taking part in the battles of Cambrai and Vimy Ridge although never firing a shot in anger. Most of his time on the front line was spent as a stretcher bearer, collecting wounded comrades, often under heavy fire, and burying the dead. It was there that the 15 years old Billy learned how to judge the quality of a man and how the horrors of war sifted the men from the boys.

In 1921, not being happy with his lot in Canada and craving the life of a travelling showman, Billy worked his passage on a cattle ship bound for England. Arriving in Liverpool with just £5 in his pocket (£170 today), he hitch hiked to Dorney's yard in Bristol to find his fairground relatives. This was where travelling showmen 'wintered', repairing and refurbishing their rides and stalls. They immediately told him that he didn't have a future in England and tried to persuade him to return to Canada. But Billy was adamant that he could make a go of it, so they eventually relented and agreed to help him, and he set up a hoopla stall which cost him thirty shillings. He beat the competition by offering bigger rings to toss round the narrow pegs and giving better prizes. Shortly after this, with help from the Hill family, Billy set up additional stalls and started to tour the summer fairs. He employed his mother on a ginger bread stall and for the next few years he travelled round the country with the fair and was so successful that, at twenty five years old, he had stalls with Bertram Mills Christmas amusements at Olympia.

He invested with Marshall Hill and progressed to other stalls and rides and quickly became a wealthy man. By the summer of 1934 he had eight successful seaside parks and seven amusement centres spread around London.

It was whilst travelling around the summer fairs that Billy became aware that the large crowds and takings that the fairgrounds had always enjoyed were beginning to dwindle. He began to realise that people had started to follow a modern craze: charabanc trips to the seaside when entire villages and factories would club together and save all year to go on a day trip to the coast. It was around this time that Billy decided that travelling had had its day and static amusements were the way forward.

Chapter Three

IT SOON BECAME OBVIOUS TO ME THAT THERE WERE a number of distractions that could affect the performance of your job as a Redcoat. There did seem to be a tremendous amount of 'frisky liaison' between the sexes and I suppose this was understandable considering there were over 1,000 young men and women working and living in such close contact. You could say that this large body of red-blooded young men and women were virtually living under the same roof. The numerous chalet parties were a nightly affair and I would say that with most of the lads, 'sleeping around' was the most popular pastime on the camp. I am not in any way sitting in judgment here. Indeed, I would say I was just as red- blooded as any and perhaps more-so than some. I just hadn't done much participating for one simple thing, I had my eye on, and wanted to get my wicked way with, the lovely Patsy Bridle!

Wilfred Orange played something of a low profile in the running of the entertainment department leaving most of it to his very capable deputy Bill Tennick who, together with the assistant manager Dave Simpson, did an excellent job. Johnny also played a big part. The reason for this was that Wilf' was Butlins dance festival organiser and was kept busy arranging the festivals at Filey and other Butlin camps. He was a very big fish in the dancing world. Dancing to big bands in big ballrooms was very popular at the end of the war and Butlins were able to provide both. Every year Wilf arranged junior dance festivals, old time, modern, Latin American and Ballroom festivals on all the Butlin camps. Wilfred introduced the weekly national Valetta competition which was judged by the resident dancing instructors, with the finals held at the Royal Albert Hall, where the floor was packed with thousands of dancers.

There were 70,000 entries at all the Butlin dance festivals and Wilf Orange can be credited with bringing thousands of bookings to Butlins every year. The first prize for a couple winning the dance festival was a £50 voucher which could be spent in the camps shops or used as deposits for future holidays. Professional dancers were forbidden to take part and all the competitors were amateurs. Butlin dance festivals were the largest in the world with competitors coming from as far away as Africa, Australia, Russia and Finland. A number of camps up until the mid-1960s had two large ballroom that were ideal for the dance festivals. Filey would have modern dance competitions in the Viennese ballroom, in some years with music played by the Teddy Foster orchestra, and at the same time Fred Percival would be playing for old time and modern sequence in the Regency. Also Butlins held young and juvenile ballroom dance festivals for ages ranging from the under-fives. One of the youngest dancing competitors was four years old and one of the oldest was over eighty. Butlins also held the British and World Ballet, Tap and Modern Dance Championships on one camp every year, with dancers aged from ten to seventeen. In the highland dance festival there is a section for the under-fives, the youngest competitor was three-and-a -half years old. Wilf retired in the late 1970s and the festivals were taken over by Roger Billington.

In a much smaller way reunion dances were featured in towns throughout great Britain. People who had holidayed at Butlins would attend to meet the Redcoats and enjoy again some of the some of the fun they'd shared during the summer.

I quickly became aware of the importance of the departments views on good time keeping and why this point was so strongly stressed. If a Redcoat was detailed for a competition and there were 30 or so entries, and he or she turned up late, that large number of people would be kept waiting I could see that this would have a snowball effect and it could prevent those kept waiting getting to the next event on time. There were certain rules and regulations and, although discussed in a pleasant way, they were rigidly enforced.

STANDING INSTRUCTIONS TO REDCOATS
General notes on dress

a) A name badge is provided, to be worn on the top edge of the blazer breast pocket. Wear it with pride - and wear it with a smile!

b) Males to wear a black bow tie (not provided) from evening meal onwards.

c) Shorts (not provided) may be worn on outside events, but for presentations i.e competitions, theatre duties etc, and from evening meal onwards white trousers/skirts must be worn.

d) Females to wear white ankle socks (not provided) when

white tennis shoes are worn.

e) Track suits will only be worn by staff designated by the entertainment manager.

f) Never wear a Mack indoors.

Do not wear: Hats, Ribbons, Hair Bands, Necklaces or Costume Jewellery.

Lifeguards: Regulation dress of full issue track suit or special vest and tracksuit bottoms must be worn at all time when on duty.

Do not wear: Jeans or other clothing restrictive to movement in an emergency.

In the Guests Dining Room, lifeguards must wear either full track suit, track suit top with white shorts, or tracksuit top with white trousers. The red vest and/or swimwear is not acceptable.

REDS MUST LOOK AFTER ISSUE CLOTHING: IT IS IN YOUR CHARGE

REMEMBER:

As a Redcoat you are a host or hostess and as such you behave exactly as if you were host in your own home to any guests who may be there. This consists of being good-mannered, knowing where everything is, to direct those who do not know, <u>mixing with as many guests as possible and not</u> <u>remaining with any one person or persons for too long.</u>

Try to take an interest in whatever you are doing. This will make your job easier and more satisfying. Being a Redcoat really boils down to having good manners and using them with common sense.

Smile and the world smiles with you moan and you'll moan at home

RETURN KEYS AND EQUIPMENT
Return keys & equipment you have drawn immediately after the event.

Return the key to the Sports Hut immediately after the Donkey Derby.

During the Winter Season you may find yourself in the middle of the Sahara Desert with the sun blazing down and the heat unbearable, you will take out your handkerchief to mop your fevered brow and a small glistening object will drop at your feet. As you stoop to pick it out of the sand you will see that it's the Sports Hut key and no use to anybody in the middle of the Sahara desert!!

POINTS TO WATCH ON SPECIAL DUTIES
BALLROOM

a) Mix with as many guests as possible. Do not single out the young and attractive partners all the time - think of the lonely guests especially the elderly ones.
b) Organize guests in Party Dances.
c) Do not congregate in groups of Redcoats.
d) Never dance with staff and always prevent men from dancing together.
e) Use your discretion when smoking.

DINING HALL
a) Be at the Dining Hall early talk to anyone at the doors.
b) Meal times are duties. Be there even if you don't want a meal.
c) Do not impede a waitress in her duties.
e) Do not enter the Dining Hall in front of the guests waiting at the door.
f) If your allocated seat is taken, always obtain another through a supervisor.

g) Moving around the Dining Hall talking to guests is called 'Swanning' you should Swan for at least five minutes before sitting down for your own meal.
h) When making champagne or birthday presentations do not impede service.
i) Remain at the table allocated to you.
j) Do remember shorts are not acceptable at the evening meal.
k) Never run in a dining room.

THEATRE DUTIES

a) The Redcoat detailed as I/C Front of the House is responsible for :-
1) Positioning the other Redcoats on Theatre Duty to best advantage on entrances, exits and gangways.
2) Ensuring door are closed when theatre is full. Checking signs and notices of next performance. Checking Baby Crying Board.
b) Ensure the doors and aisles are not blocked by pushchairs and wheelchairs. Do not leave the theatre until a full fire check has been completed.

COMPETITION RESULTS

a) Always fill in a proper competition result form. Include Christian name and all details. Always fill in the "Age" as this is an important guide for the Hostess who has to provide a suitable prize. You need not embarrass anyone by asking their age - assess it as near as possible.

ALL DETAILS TO BE ENTERED IN CAPITAL LETTERS

b) having completed the above form, sign it and hand it in at the office without delay.
c) Never tell a guest what they are likely to receive as a prize.

FINAL POINTS ON MATTERS THAT WILL BE HELPFUL TO YOU

1) Always carry your "Daily Detail"- To 'not know' is not an excuse.
2) If the detail differs from the programme, check with the office - if this is not possible then go by your detail.

No event is ever cancelled

3) if an event doesn't run announce it as "postponed" and 'plug' the alternative event.
4) Use your own common sense about smoking, the general rule however is no smoking on duty.
5) Do not linger in the bars too long. Fifteen minutes is the maximum and mix around. Sit with guests when in uniform.

We don't want bar flies.

6) Know "What's on" and "Where". Don't just memorise your own duties but acquaint yourself with the programme and amenities as a whole. You will look rather foolish if asked something by a guest and you have to reply "I don't know"
7) Do not switch duties without permission of the Entertainment Manager, his Deputy or the Chief Redcoat.
8) Be courteous to other departmental staff - we are working for the same Company. Should you experience difficulty with the staff of another Department, refer it to your own manager who can deal with it far more

effectively than you.
9) Refer any complaint direct to the House Chairman. Always be sympathetic

BUT DO NOT AGREE OR COMMIT YOURSELF

Make a note of the complaint and the name and chalet number of the guest and refer it to the office.
10) Do not accept Lost Property refer the finder to the Lost Property

DO BE AWARE

Your manager is here to protect your interests as well as to supervise your work so, if you have any troubles put in a request to see him. Remember you are never fully dressed without a smile. Be happy in your job 'Mix & Mingle' and 'Smile' as you do it. The guests will show you respect and affection - give it back!! Buses and trains run late - Butlin Redcoats are always on time! If things get tough remember the saying "You Said You Could Do It When You Wrote In"

Chapter Four

I HAD HEARD THAT SOME ONE INVOLVED WITH the production of the Redcoat show wasn't happy with the Opening and had called a rehearsal to put the problem right. I had also learned that these rehearsals were always held at midnight, as that was the only time everyone involved could come together. I decided to go along for the experience. The boxing instruction finished at five o'clock and Harry and I had started being detailed for the Viennese ballroom in the evenings. Johnny had explained that we were also GD Redcoats and so that was expected of us. We were both happy with the arrangement as it made us feel more a part of things as we felt a bit isolated in the boxing marquee. Harry had to attend the rehearsal anyway as, having started two weeks before me, he was in the show. The dancing finished at eleven o'clock and so like a number of others we arrived at the theatre early.

I had never been involved in anything like it before so I didn't know what to expect. At midnight the Redcoats were called on stage and Johnny and Maurice one of the compere's started to explain what was wrong with the routine. The Reds went off stage to the left and right. Johnny stayed back stage as he was in the opening but Maurice came down into the auditorium. He had a quick word with an organist, the only musician in the pit, who started to play a few bars of introduction to a number I knew called "That's Entertainment" There was a microphone at each side of the stage and Billy Miller and Kathy Merrick took one each, they were both in red and whites and I had seen them entertaining in the bars as 'Miller & Merrick'. Billy started to sing:-

Billy	The costumes the scenery, the make up the props. The audience that lifts you when you're down
Kathy	The headaches, the heartaches, the backaches the flops. The sheriff who escorts you out of town
Billy	The Opening when your heart beats like a drum"
Kathy	The closing when the audience won't come"

The Redcoats entered from both sides of the stage and were in boy following girl order. They came on stage brightly and all smiling.

All	There's no business like show business,
	like no business I know
Lads	Everything about it is appealing
Girls	Everything the traffic will allow
Lads	Nowhere could you have that happy feeling
All	Like when you're stealing that extra bow.
	There's no people like show people,
	They smile when they are low.
Lads	Yesterday they told you would not go far
Girls	That night you opened and there you are
Lads	Next day on your dressing room they've hung a star
All	Let's go on with the show. Let's Go On with the Show!!

The hair was standing up on the back of my neck and I was trembling with excitement. Somehow I just had to be a part of that. If there was a problem with the show then it was something I had missed because I couldn't fault it. I thought it was superb and every single person on stage had, in my book at least, been absolutely first-class. They had all been in step, smiling broadly and what a sight, fifteen lads and fifteen good looking girls and all of them in red and white - what a picture. Johnny came off stage to have a whispered conversation with Maurice, who it appeared, had also been pleased with what he had seen.

They spoke in low tones, I wasn't eavesdropping, but I got the gist of it and gathered they were putting whatever the problem had been down to nerves caused by a live audience. But, as everyone was present and available, they ran it through a couple more times. After seeing it for a second time I felt confident that I could do it and had a word with Maurice but he pointed out that I would be an odd number. He also said that some of the campers who knew me would wonder why I was in the Opening and not the Finale. They were valid reasons of course which I accepted but it just made me even more determined that one day I would become a part of it all. However, all was not doom and gloom. One of the stage crew had made an urn of tea and Harry, who had seen me chatting to Maurice, had got me a cup. He was sitting on the front row with Johnny and he beckoned me to join them. There was an empty seat next to mine and it was suddenly filled by the gorgeous Patsy Bridle.

We didn't need an introduction as we had met and spoken briefly on a couple of occasions. This was Patsy's third season and so she knew Harry and Johnny quite well. Johnny took me to one side to ask me for a favour. He explained that his brother Dave was a Redcoat at the Skegness camp and had asked to borrow a blank pistol from him. It appeared that he need it for an act he was doing. Johnny explained that apart from the weight there were other problems involved in sending a pistol and ammunition through the post. I was one of the few members of staff who had a car and Johnny asked me if I would take him to Skegness and I was pleased to agree. We had by this time been joined by Ronnie the Geordie pianist who said he would like to come along for the ride. After chatting with Harry we agreed that a Monday would be the best day for doing this. It was around 2. O'clock when our midnight gathering finished so I offered to walk Patsy back to her chalet. My reward for doing this was a gentle but friendly peck on the cheek, I consoled myself with the thought that every relationship has to start somewhere and, at least, we had linked arms walking through the camp!

During my short time in red and whites I had developed a desire to get more involved in the activities of a general duty Redcoat. I had seen them with their house floats on the Sunday morning march past. This was when the musicians of various orchestra's would amalgamate to form one big marching band and lead a parade around the camp. I had seen teams of them with their house captains and large crowds of campers having fun on the house group photographs. They also trained teams for inter-house ball games, which were held during a session of fun and games on Friday mornings.

The GD Redcoats organised and ran all the competitions snooker, billiards, table tennis, darts and every other item in the programme.

They also 'dressed' the major competitions in the ballroom and organised the campers on Sports Day and the Swimming Gala. They seemed to spend every waking moment having fun and mixing with the campers and I felt that I was somehow missing out. They had included me in the Friday night Au Revoir in the ball room and I'd had no problem with that. Two of the girls had talked me through it and it was a piece of cake. I hadn't known the words to 'Goodnight Campers' and so I'd mimed it, no one had noticed, and I had learned them now.

On Monday morning I went to meet Johnny and Ronnie

on the car park and was sitting in the car letting the engine tick over when the boys arrived. I couldn't believe my luck! With them was Patsy Bridle!! The boys sat in the back and I was in the front with the gorgeous Patsy. I found that most of the Redcoats, by nature of the job they chose to do, were fun people and always up for a laugh. My three passengers were no different in fact zanier than most and we had a laugh- a- minute journey to Skegness. I mentioned to the boys that I had been amused by the names given to some of the characters in the Old Time Music Hall, Eileen Dover, Lucy Lastic, Teresa Green, and Lydia Dustbin. They told me that those names had been made up by the two of them and they then proceeded to tell us, with shrieks of laughter from me and Patsy, of names they had come up with but couldn't use!…Neil & Blomee.. Al Beefhooked.. Arfur Foulksake ….Anita Handjob….. Ben Timover!!

Whilst not quite as big as Filey, Skegness was a large camp and at a guess I would say it's camper capacity was not far off the numbers that we could accommodate. Like Filey it had two enormous ballrooms, but I also saw it had the advantage of two outdoor swimming pools. The bars were similar and it had a Pig and Whistle, each ballroom also had a bar and I gathered that the Empress Bar was the main sing-song and bar show venue. The theatre was a different story altogether and I was informed that until recent years it had been open to the general public. The Stage Manager also told me that it had been built for no less than Adolf Hitler, designed as an amphitheatre, but with a roof, and it had been the showpiece at the Glasgow World Fair in 1938. There were no pillars in the auditorium and the stage could be seen from every seat in the theatre. The illuminated proscenium arch was out of this world and, I was also informed, larger than the one at the London Palladium.

We had gone to the theatre to see Johnny's brother Dave who, before moving to Skegness, had been a Filey Redcoat the previous year. Old hands at Filey had told me he was a very talented comedian. He was now doing a double act with fellow Redcoat Al Page. It was an unusual act and in my view rather strange. They both did a zany Jerry Lewis impersonation! Each had the famous Jerry Lewis trademark and wore their hair in a crew cut. There was no doubt that their impersonation was very good, and I couldn't decide if one was better than the other, but it seemed strange to have two men on stage together and both impersonating the same person! The journey back to

Filey was just as pleasurable as the one going out but also rewarding in more ways than one. The trip gave me an opportunity to talk to Johnny about my desire for more involvement. He didn't hesitate and immediately agreed that my general duties could be extended further than just the ballroom.

I knew that the chief Redcoat allocated the Redcoat's their duties in what was called a "Daily Detail" and Johnny promised that he would detail me for a variety of duties in the evening. This would involve the Gaiety Theatre, with the revue and variety shows, the Playhouse Theatre for repertory plays, and the Empire for family film shows.. He asked me if I would like the odd session on the bingo and of course I said I would.

The trip had also been successful for a number of reasons. I had seen another camp and learned a bit more about Butlins. I had started friendships with Johnny and Ronnie and most important I had got on famously with Patsy who, during the trip had enthused about a local beauty spot called Robin Hoods Bay, which we had agreed to visit together on our next day off.

Johnny, true to his word, started putting me on a variety of details which I absolutely loved and I started feeling much more like a Butlin Redcoat. It also gave me an opportunity to watch some of the Redcoats perform. Some of them did warm-ups in the theatre about 20 minutes before the start of the show. At first I thought the gags and material they used was their own particular 'spot' or gimmick but I quickly learned that they were set routines often used by different Redcoats. During the first few days I saw Jeff Whitfield, do a routine that I thought was quite amusing. "Right, I want everyone in the theatre to clasp hands with the person sitting each side of you. Come on now clasp hands. Those on the end of the row reach over the aisle to hold hands with the person across the aisle. If you're in an end seat turn round and clasp hands with the person sitting behind. That's right I want you in one long snake right round the theatre." He now pointed a finger to the back of the theatre "Right, I'm now speaking to the gentleman in the white shirt at the back of the theatre. Yes, you Sir, keep holding hands but please stand up. That's right. Now reach behind you…. And Put Your Finger In That Light Socket!!" It got a ripple and I thought it was a novel couple of minutes. The following week I saw the girl called Bingo Betty doing a warm-up and she used exactly the same routine. I saw a few other little 'snippets' shared by some of the others over the weeks. I asked one of the seasoned Redcoats about this and he explained that there had been a Redcoat comedian at Filey a couple of years ago and he had introduced them. When he left for pastures new they had been filched by the Redcoats and no-one could lay claim to them. You just had to make sure that someone hadn't used it before you in the same week. There was another " Right everyone shake hands with the person sitting on your left. That's lovely, say hello. Now shake hands with the person on your right. Go on say hello. Now I want you to do this nice and quickly. Turn round and shake hands with the person behind you!" This of course couldn't be done because when a person turned to shake hands the person sitting behind had also turned to shake hands. There was another that could be used by the Redcoats doing warm-ups as often as they wanted. Almost everyone smoked in those days even in the theatres and most people carried matches or a lighter.

The following was popular if someone was celebrating a birthday. "Now ladies and gentlemen, I was told just before I came on stage that we are celebrating a birthday tonight. Tonight in the audience we have little Mandy Smith, and today Mandy is eight years old.

We are going to make an enormous birthday cake for Mandy so everybody take out a match or your cigarette lighter. When I count to three I would like you all to light them and the stage manager will dim the theatre lights. ONE, TWO, THREE!!.... To see over a thousand lighters or matches suddenly spring to light in a darkened theatre was an impressive sight-especially for eight year old Mandy!

There were other gimmicks shared by the Redcoats and one was to split the theatre into two halves or parts and nominate a couple of Redcoats for each part. Then get them to sing different songs at the same time. Johnny O'Mahoney was absolutely first class doing warm-ups and none of the others could come anywhere near him for sheer personality and magnetism. Of course Johnny was superb in everything he did and the campers absolutely adored him. He could be the sophisticated Irish intellectual one minute and the total clown the next. He was handsome, charming and flamboyant. The ideal ingredients for a perfect Redcoat and of which Johnny was the epitome. It was said "When they were making Redcoats, God made Johnny O'Mahoney and then he broke the mould."

Patsy and I had become an item, I had discretely moved into her chalet and we were seeing each every spare minute. Whenever

I took Johnny to see his brother at Skegness, Patsy came and often Ronnie would come too. The Entertainment Manager at Skegness was Frank Mansell and I always dropped in at his office to pay my respects. I had noticed that the Redcoat blazers at Skeggy were a vast improvement on the ones we had at Filey. The braid round the lapels and cuffs was blue-ours was black. There blazers were better cut than ours and had shoulder pads and a half lining. I asked Mr Mansell about this and he told me that the Skegness Redcoats had been issued with what would eventually be the new style for all the camps. They weren't being issued en masse but in batches and other camps would get them eventually.

Johnny at one of the Redcoat meetings advised us that a number of Redcoats would be detailed for a rather unusual but very special event. It would be the arrival on the camp of 'Big Charlie' who was an Indian male tusker with the reputation of being the largest elephant in the world. He weighed eight and a half tons, stood over twelve feet high and was thirteen feet long. Big Charlie's Butlin career had first started at the Ayr camp in Scotland, where the campers and the children loved him and his mahout Ibrahim. He was such an enormous success with everyone that Billy decided that he should be on one of the larger camps. The nearest large camp to Ayr was of course Filey, the flagship of the fleet. But how was Big Charlie to be moved? The distance was almost 400 miles.

Billy Butlin knew that moving Big Charlie would make a lot of newspaper headlines and so in his usual fashion he started to milk it for all it was worth. He began by putting adverts in the national newspapers.

Butlins Holiday Camps will pay the sum of £1,000 cash to any person who can arrange immediate and safe transport of the largest elephant in captivity from Butlins Ayr (Scotland) to Butlins Filey (Yorkshire) please apply to Butlins Luxury Holliday Camps, Oxford Street, London W1.

Eventually it was decided that the best method was to move him in a gigantic crate made from nine-inch thick railway sleepers securely bolted to iron girders, built on a low-loader. Once inside his feet would have to be securely tethered with heavy metal chains. I did hear that it took his mahout Shaik Ibrahim twenty four hours to entice him aboard. Evidently they could not fasten his trunk as an elephant will be driven crazy if he can't move his trunk and the last thing you would want on the back of a low-loader is a peed off eight ton elephant! It was thought that when inside the crate Big Charlie might decide to rub himself up against the walls. Strong as the sleepers were, he could just possibly burst them. Someone suggested rubbing the walls with lard. Ibrahim overheard this suggestion and went potty "Ibrahim will no go in box and if Ibrahim no go in box, Charlie no go in box! Pig fat, Ibrahim no touch!" It was then realised that it was against his religion to touch pig fat.

Eventually, to massive press coverage, the journey started and it would eventually take six days. The publicity was tremendous and that alone must have been worth far more than Billy's offer of £1,000 to do the move. I was told that a crowd of some 5,000 people gathered on the sports field to see the arrival of Big Charlie. It had taken Ibrahim 24 hours to get him in the 'crate' but Charlie must have settled down and felt at home because now the mahout couldn't get him out! It eventually took four hours and three sacks of apples to entice him from the trailer!

I began to realise that sadly my first season as a Butlin Redcoat was drawing to a close but, when I reflected on that, I realised that I had come a long way in such short time. I had achieved what I had hoped for and was now doing more work as a GD Redcoat, which meant getting amongst the campers far more than I was when restricted to boxing and ballroom duties. I had learned a lot from my duties in the Gaiety Theatre, simply watching the Redcoats doing warm-ups and having fun with their party pieces. I had also learned by watching the artistes on the shows and had picked up a few theatrical expressions and phrases along the way I knew what was meant by "From the top" - I knew the difference between "Up stage and upstage" - I knew where the 'Wings' were and the difference between a Proscenium and a Cyclorama. I knew that "Dead Segue" meant 'Straight in'.

I was becoming a proper little 'Lovey' and I wallowed in it. I had even compered a couple of early evening quiz shows and on a couple of occasions Betty Bingo had let me use the microphone to call a house. She had kindly pointed out to me when I was too near the mic' and sounding muffled or too far away and couldn't be clearly heard. I had learned from Betty that the microphone was an instrument and like all instruments it had to be played correctly. Frankly I couldn't have had a better teacher! I was proud of the fact that I hadn't let the side down by neglecting the boxing. That is what I had been engaged to do and I had done it to the very best of my ability. I had arranged for the week to culminate on Friday evening, in a one hour session of boxing exhibitions. Ken, Harry and I would find a suitable opponent during the week and each of us would do three x 3 minute rounds of exhibition boxing. This of course was as good, bad or indifferent as the boxers who happened to be with us. Some weeks someone with a bit of experience would turn up and we could spend a few rounds sparring and preparing something for the exhibition.

But I have to admit that mostly they were just keen amateurs looking for ten minutes of limelight in front of their mates. I had genuinely devoted my every attention to the training and sparring between ten o'clock in the morning and the last session finishing at five o'clock in the afternoon. Johnny and I had become good friends. I appreciated his enormous comedy talent and ability on a microphone and I think Johnny, as chief red, liked my reliability. Our trips to Skegness had become a regular fortnightly affair and we'd had the opportunity to get to know each and our friendship had grown. When I knew the exhibitions weren't going to be strong I would welcome Johnny's introduction of a bit of comedy. Under normal circumstances the sessions would be refereed by Tommy Cassidy, a former Scottish champion, and the manager of the Viennese Ballroom.

When the standard wasn't too high Johnny would referee and some of his comedy was outrageous. When giving the boxers instructions in the centre of the ring he would suddenly open an opponent's gloves to expose two large iron bolts. He had a rubber hammer which he used if the boxers didn't break when instructed. Ken was usually in the final exhibition and in the last round he would feign being beaten and would go down. Johnny would start to count but, too much laughter, there would be a five second space between each second he called. Harry and I would remain ringside still with gloves on and Johnny would push us through the ropes to join in with Ken. We would slap Ken's opponent but with open gloves. It looked very effective and Johnny would join in hitting him with the rubber hammer. Pure slapstick but the crowd loved it and it was more entertaining than sitting through an hour of mediocre boxing.

I felt that I had become a much better Redcoat by just watching Johnny and some of the others and I was desperately keen to start doing some of the things I had seen them do. I was determined to contact Wilfred Orange before the start of next season and ask to come back on general duties. I felt that I'd had a good season and never been even a minute late for any event. He had often dropped in on the instruction and exhibitions and thanked me for what he had seen. Towards the end of the season the weeks seemed to simply fly by and I was to discover that the happiness of starting a season can only be equalled by the sadness of it coming to an end. I suddenly realised with just a few days to go that certain plans I had been formulating had to now be put into effect. During my first Butlin season I had come to realise that this was what I wanted to do in life. I loved the job and the Butlin way of life but I knew that I didn't yet have either the talent or the experience to get winter work within the Entertainment Department.

Talking to some of the others I had been told that usually just a few Redcoats were retained for work during the winter at one, or another, of the Butlin hotels. I was informed that the company had hotels at Bognor, Margate and Blackpool. I guessed that Johnny and Ronnie would be offered winter work and I was right in my prediction, in a couple of days we would learn that both Johnny and Ronnie were going to the Butlin Ocean Hotel at Brighton.

On a couple of occasions Big Ken, Harry and I had been required to break up fights in the Viennese Ballroom. These were usually caused by drunken youths on Friday nights. The lads involved had seen us in the ring sparring and doing exhibitions and so they knew who we were.

This meant that we were usually able to stop the fights without resorting to violence. The Camp Controller was a nice, gentlemanly sort of man called Eric Bennett, who had witnessed some of these incidents and expressed his appreciation.

I knew that maintenance staff were kept on throughout the winter to do a variety of jobs around the camp and, although I was not trained for any trade in particular, I was adaptable and felt that I was up to this. I asked his secretary to make an appointment for me to see him. I had my interview with Eric Bennett and was delighted with the outcome. He listened to my request and immediately offered me a job. He then passed me over to his deputy Harry Hutchinson to discuss the details. He told me there was a big painting programme afoot and that at least twelve painters would be working on the project. I gathered the plan was to paint every single stick of furniture on the entire staff camp. With around 800 people living on those lines, this figure excluded Redcoats who lived in camper chalets and didn't include local 'Live Out' staff, and presuming the main occupancy was two people to a chalet, 400 was still a lot of chalets. Each chalet would have a bed, chest of drawers, chair, and wardrobe and so it was also a lot of furniture. It seemed that Billy Butlin had decreed that all the furniture should now become 'Butlin blue'. Billy had his own paint Company called "Beaver Paints". He had named this particular shade of blue 'Butlin blue' as it was his favourite colour. Harry Hutchinson told me that I wouldn't be on a set wage and it was a piece rate job. When he told me the rates it didn't really tell me a great deal as I had no idea how much painting could be done in a week.

The rates were:
1 shilling a chair. ………. ……….(5p)
2 shillings a wardrobe………… ..(10p)
Half a crown a double bed …… (12.5p)

    I was told that everything had to be brush painted and that rollers, a new invention that didn't properly cover, could not be used. I had become friendly with Wally the supervisor in the clothing store and he kindly let me have a set of white painter's overalls. I would be provided with paint brushes and paint and so I was all set to go.

    I got lodgings with a jolly lady called Mrs Baker, in Rutland street. The accommodation was found for me by Marjory Tennick, the Radio Butlin supervisor, who was also the wife of Bill the deputy entertainment manager.

    Saying goodbye to good friends was pretty painful as, working in such a close relationship, some very strong friendships were forged. Patsy, Harry and Johnny had all pledged to come back next season so it was only a separation for a few months. We all promised to write as people didn't phone much in those days.

    I had been told that the department always arranged a fantastic all night, 'End of Season Party' which I gathered was a Butlin tradition from way back and done on all the camps. Johnny and Ronnie asked if I had any ideas for a party piece and I gathered that the Redcoats got themselves into small teams to provide a bit of entertainment. There was evidently a different theme for the party every year and this year it was to be a Christmas party. Patsy and

Marjory, the Radio Butlin supervisor had persuaded a local baker to make them mince pies and I knew half a dozen were rehearsing carols. The fact that I had been asked to do something with Johnny and Ronnie pleased me and so I gave it a quite a bit of thought and eventually came up with something I thought would at least be appropriate. Johnny and Ronnie liked it and agreed that the three of us would sing it together.

(To the tune of)   <u>GOOD KING WENCESLAS</u>

Mister Tennick last looked out, on the feast of season,
When the Recoats stood about , looking crisp and even,
Loudly swore the boss that night, like a London coster
When he found one of the Redcoats missing from his roster,
Hither Johnny stand by me, if thou knowest spill it,
This here Redcoat who is he, where the hell's his billet?

Boss he lives a good league hence, his name is Pat O'Malley.
He'll be getting slowly sloshed in his ruddy chalet.
Out into the snow they went, forth they went together,
Through the crude winds wild lament, typical Filey weather.

"Bill the night is darker now and the wind blows stronger,
It makes me fart I know not how, I can't go on much longer."
Keep on going Johnny lad and you will not rue it,
Don't Forget When You Wrote In
YOU SAID THAT YOU COULD DO IT!!

Ronnie played it on piano and the three of us sang it to a good response from the Reds. It developed into something of an all-night shindig, especially with some of the lads. Patsy and I slipped away around three in the morning and were told the following day that it was still going strong at six. With the Stage Manager Joe and his crew still drinking as they cleared up. Of course, they didn't have to worry about Redcoat duties!

I managed to see the first performance of the Friday night Redcoat Show, before I went on ballroom duty and, as we had all expected, it was a real tear jerking affair. At the end of the Finale the Redcoats just threw their arms around each other with every single girl genuinely sobbing her heart out. Patsy told me it was even more heart-rending on the second house. The final Au Revoir was more sorrowful still, with even the boys and the campers joining in and weeping, there wasn't a dry eye in the place. It's not hard to imagine the strong feelings of emotion that build up in a team of close friends who have spent a long, fun-packed summer together, having to say goodbye for the winter and, in some cases perhaps forever. We all said our farewells in our own particular way then, like the proverbial ships passing in the night, we parted company for the winter. That brought to an end my first Butlin season and to say I had enjoyed every single moment of it would be the greatest understatement ever made. Staying on at Filey had a number of benefits. I was still with the company that I loved and it would enable me to get to know Butlins and the camp so much better and I would also get the opportunity to meet and make friends with lots of work mates on the permanent staff.

Chapter Five

MRS BAKER WAS A SWEET AND MOTHERLY WOMAN who had lived in Filey all her sixty odd years but had never once been on the camp. She always gave me a nice cooked breakfast, provided me with a sandwich lunch and I could look forward to an excellent meal in the evening.

Part of my duties in the summer, with a small team of other Redcoats, had been to collect waste paper and litter on the amusement park and, this was done on Friday nights. The manager Alf Roberts and his assistant John Norris were a couple of decent blokes but absolutely fanatical that you picked up every single lolly stick. God forbid if you missed one. "Rocky you've missed three lolly sticks over here! I'll kick your arse." It was all done in fun and with a laugh of course. They were both keen boxing fans and seemed to take it in turns to come to the Friday exhibitions. During the winter they had a workshop on the park and a kettle to make tea and they also had the facilities to wash paint brushes.

On my first day in my new profession of furniture painter they invited me to have my lunch in their workshop. Within a very short time I had decided that I couldn't afford to take tea breaks and couldn't take much time off at all if I was to make the job pay. I had done my sums after a couple of days and realised that I would be lucky if, as they say in Yorkshire, I was able to make ends meet. The rates they were paying just weren't high enough. The furniture was in assorted colours red, green and orange and all of it needed two coats. If I found something already in Butlin blue it was a bonus as I could mix together a drop of undercoat and gloss and get away with one coat.

On the Wednesday afternoon, to ensure I would earn enough wages to at least pay my rent, I had to collect all the blue furniture I could find and spend the rest of the week painting that, giving it one coat but charging for two. I told Alf and John about my problem and my fears that I might have to give the job up. The following day John came looking for me to ask if I could get access to the key cupboard where the keys were kept. I was able to tell him that I had both the key to the cupboard and the key to the staff accommodation office as I was going to have to work the weekend.

Cappy the staff accommodation manager had loaned me a set of keys as he would be off duty. Late on Friday Alf asked me to let him have the keys. I was a bit surprised at this but didn't ask any questions. I had been allocated a complete chalet line of back-to-back chalets and told to paint the furniture contents. On Saturday morning, when I looked in the next one that I was due to paint, I was surprised and delighted to see that it contained nothing but Butlin blue furniture and on checking I found that so did all the rest on my line.

Alf and John had got their staff to swap over all my furniture with that on other lines and replace it with Butlin blue. They had also mixed me a special blend of paint that consisted of gloss, undercoat and a touch of high gloss varnish. Just one coat gave my furniture a very professional finish and in one kindly act by Alf and John my wages had been doubled, my bacon had been saved and I could stay on at Filey camp. That was the start of a very pleasant and happy winter for me in dear old Filey.

I was living just around the corner from Bill and Marjory and at the weekend they took me for a guided tour of some of the delightful pubs around the village. I bought a second hand fishing rod and spent a few pleasant Sunday afternoons, with Don Haddington, a young electrician on the camp, fishing off Filey Brigg.

The Brigg is an enormous rock about 10 metres high at its apex. It's possible to climb down an iron ladder to a more acceptable fishing position on a sea-level platform of rock. It is alleged that on the Brigg was once a Roman Signal Station and excavations found five large stones believed to be altars, a dog chasing a stag is carved on one of them. The stones can now be seen in Filey Crescent Gardens.

Having a car made getting to and from work much easier as, in the winter season, the local bus service wasn't too frequent. I had no trouble finding four lads who were more than happy to be given a lift to and from the camp. They contributed quite fairly towards the petrol and from their point of view being four in number it was much cheaper than the bus fare, also more convenient, and a better ride. Everyone on the camp had to clock in and out at the main gate and so that became our dropping off and pick up point.

I was now making a reasonable wage, didn't need to work weekends and could slow down a bit. I had watched a painter on the camp paint a door with a five inch latex foam roller and he did it five times faster than with a brush. It would be ideal for flat wardrobes and chests of drawers. I obtained one and kept it hidden in a sandwich box, concealing the handle behind a wardrobe. It made my earning power greater still, although hiding my equipment made me feel like a cat burglar but it greatly increased my wages. I could now afford a nice social life in the evenings and on weekends. When the winter came it was bitterly cold and having no form of heating in the chalets where I was painting made the job more than a bit uncomfortable. But the winter was passing, some weeks, it seemed, more slowly than others, but it was passing. I made a lot of new friends in Filey and was persuaded to join the Imperial Inn's darts team, it was the second team and not in a league so we didn't have to be too serious and we had a lot of laughs. Suddenly we were well into a New Year and the opening of the camp was getting ever nearer.

    I had started to meet some very interesting characters around the camp and to enable me to spend time with them I was now using the staff canteen more frequently for my lunch break. They had fascinating stories to tell. Norman Bradford and Frank Cusworth were two of the original Redcoat team which had been formed in 1936 at the opening of Skegness, and by coincidence they had both been engineers and had worked on Billy's parks before the camp was built. They both new him well and I noticed they always referred to him as 'The Guv'nor'. They would enthrall me with their stories and especially so when talking about the old days. Because of my love for the job I had developed a tremendous interest in the company and had become an avid reader of everything Butlin. During the season I had acquired a copy of one of the many books written about the 'Butlin Story' and had naturally accepted the contents as factual. But when I discussed certain points with either Frank or Norman they would dismiss most of it as "That's just a complete load of rubbish!"

    The book contained an account of Billy being asked to leave a boarding house after breakfast and I told them that the book said "Billy Butlin first nurtured the idea of a holiday camp because he had seen landladies literally push families out of boarding houses between meals" Frank in a nice way said "Rocky that's nonsense as well and I'll tell you exactly why he opened his first camp". He went on to explain to me that as early as 1925 Billy had a static amusement park at Barry Island and he had joined him when he built another at Skegness. Both sites contained penny arcades, an hoopla stall, a tower slide, scenic railway and haunted house. He continued to expand at Skegness and by 1930 it included a zoo featuring six zebras, four lions, three dancing bears, a leopard, a kangaroo, several monkeys, seals and an entire African village which in those days was an enormous attraction. Norman told me that halfway round the attractions was a sign that said "This Way To The EGRET" unfortunately it was quite close to a door leading out of the zoo and quite a number of visitors left the park. An 'Egret' is actually a type of White Heron, with fine plumes and long feathers that cascade down an Egrets back. The zoo visitors thought Egret was 'Exit' and left without seeing half the attractions.

By 1932 he had opened a similar park at Bognor with kangaroos, polar bears and monkeys and by 1935 most of his amusement parks had zoos attached to them which produced additional revenue. Both Frank and Norman refuted the suggestion in the book that Billy made his millions from the camps and Frank said "Let me tell you, Billy Butlin was a millionaire long before the camps. That stuff about going cap-in-hand and begging to borrow money is claptrap!"

Between them they went on to tell me that by the 1930s the Butlin zoos, amusement parks and fairgrounds stretched as far as Barry, Bognor, Skegness, Mabletorpe, Hayling Island, Felixstowe, Southsea, The Isle of Man and Sheerness. I was told that his time as a stall holder with Marshall Hill was very short lived and by 1925 he had his own travelling fair. Frank continued "By the time I joined he'd acquired the sole rights in Great Britain for Dodgem cars and had it well sewn up. If other showmen wanted them they had to hire them from him and that was on a 50/50 share basis!! Bank managers were almost coming to borrow money from him I'll tell you!!"

Rather than a ruthless Barry landlady being his inspiration behind the camps the truth was that he found his static amusement parks were making far more money than his travelling fair which was touring the length and breadth of the country. His static parks didn't incur petrol costs for the large number of vehicles needed to travel, no wages for extra men continually erecting and taking down the rides. They told me that Billy started to toy with the idea of an enormous amusement park, or centre, providing accommodation, dining rooms and further facilities that would encourage holiday-makers to stay on the site. I realised these were the true facts and I wasn't getting them from a publicist trying to establish an image, this was coming straight from the horse's mouth! I just wallowed in the company of these old

Butlin pioneers.

I had frequently and carefully thought about my ambition to become a general duty Redcoat and the best way to go about it. I had decided that late March would be a good time to write to Wilfred Orange. I had no way of knowing that my plans and desires for the future were about to come to earth with a dreadful bump.

I had noticed a fairly extensive building programme was occurring at the side of the Gaiety building but had no idea what this annexe was going to be. The building already contained the old time ballroom, a bar, coffee bar and games room and I couldn't imagine why this large extension was being built. One day in the canteen I heard people discussing a sports stadium and I was suddenly all ears.

I listened for a while before asking any questions and when I got the answers my worst fears were confirmed. The new building was going to be just that, a stadium for boxing training and exhibitions and visiting all-star wrestling shows and it was being built to replace the old Billy Smart marquee. At first my heart was in my boots and the thought of not going on general duties was very hard to take but then common sense started to prevail. I carefully considered the situation and began to realise that over the past 15 years I had trained as a boxer and had become very proficient both as an exponent and as a trainer. I was also a fully trained former RAF physical training instructor. I had found a company that I wanted to be with and not for just one or two seasons. I had found a way of life that really suited me. Could this new stadium be a platform, a stage for me to show how good I was at what they had engaged me to do? I was good at boxing, training, instruction and exhibitions and in reality that was the best I had to offer Butlins, In the long term was the new stadium really a stroke of good fortune? I began to realise that perhaps it was. It was a large building and must have cost an absolute fortune to build and being a new project all eyes would be on it during the coming season. Perhaps this was an opportunity for me to shine!!

The weeks were rolling by and we were now enjoying some pleasant spring weather. The chalets where I was working had been dreadfully cold throughout the long winter and I had stumbled on a frightening realisation. The camp could hold around 11,000 visitors and over 1,000 members of staff. This involved hundreds of chalets and it dawned on me that the mattresses, blankets and pillows remained in the chalets right throughout the cold damp winter. Large teams of local women were engaged before the camp opened to make up the beds with freshly laundered sheets and pillow cases but the bedding couldn't be taken away to be dried out. How could it? There was such an enormous amount. It occurred to me that anyone sleeping on camp in the first week dried out their own bed by sleeping in it. Not a pleasant thought!

Coming from the city of Bradford, as I had, with its grimy, smoke stained buildings I could really appreciate the small fishing village of Filey. The place was full of wonderful characters and lots of them from fishing families who had lived in the town for generations. The Williamson's, Jenkinson's, Cappleman's and Haxby's, with nicknames like 'Little Tich', 'Big Tich,' 'Dag' and 'Galley' still braving the seas in their small coble boats to earn a modest but honest living. Countless Filey cobles, and often all their crews had been lost over the centuries. There were some definite reasons why the Filey coble was involved in disasters. When many boats were laid up for the winter the cobles were out long-line fishing - at the very time when gales were most likely. The coble is for its size, one of the safest boats afloat, but, if hit unexpectedly by very a heavy sea, it is as vulnerable as any small craft.

There was one remarkable character known as Cap'n Dave, who would spend most days in the Imperial dressed in stained corded trousers, Breton seaman's sweater, red spotted neckerchief and sporting a gold earring and numerous tattoos. Visitors would happily buy him pints to be regaled by his saga's of the sea. They would sit enthralled by his stories of shipwrecks, smuggling and piracy. I have sat with him for hours listening to his exciting tales of tall wooden ships in full sail out in Filey bay. I still continued to drink with old Cap'n Dave even after the locals assured me he was a retired thespian from Leeds who had never been to sea in his life!

It had become the custom for me to share a table in the staff canteen with Frank, Norman and another old timer Jim Batten. Jim first came to Filey in 1940 with the RAF Regiment, when the camp was known as RAF Hunmanby Moor. He had met and married a local girl and stayed on at Butlins, later becoming a maintenance manager. It was Jim who told me that the large concave mirrors on the walls of some of the buildings had been wartime searchlight reflectors. He pointed out the WD arrows on the snooker tables and explained they were ex NAAFI. He told me the camp trains taking families for joy rides round the camp and to the beach had been used during the war to take bombs to the aircraft on RAF bomber stations. He told me that for a few years after the war campers at Filey were still using RAF cutlery and crockery.

Norman and Frank had worked on the construction of Skegness camp in 1935, and it was pointed out to me that the first camp was nothing like they are today. Frank explained we had to evolve over a number of years to get to what they are now. Skegness was built to accommodate just 1,000 people in 600 chalets. It had a dining hall, games room and outdoor swimming pool. It had no theatre and when it was realised that some form of evening entertainment was required the tables in the dining room were put together to form a stage. Hughie Green of 'Opportunity Knocks' fame was appearing with a Gang Show, at the local Arcadia theatre and went to the camp to perform in the first ever Butlin show. Slowly over the years a boating lake appeared. Then tennis courts, bowling and putting greens and a cricket pitch. At the end of the year another £40,000 was invested to build a second dining hall, theatre and gymnasium and to increase the capacity to 2,000. The camp eventually went on the accommodate around 10,000 holiday makers.

The camp sewage farm was giving Billy a problem, he hadn't ever designed one before and this like many other things it had been designed on the back of a cigarette packet. Even though it was some distance away the stench was awful. Billy decided that a high fence around the sewage works might not be enough to deter the curious campers, so he put up a notice "Beware of the dog". One day a typical Yorkshire camper, in flat cap and braces approached him and pointing in the direction of the sewage said " I think tha should be told Mr Butlin, tha's got a dog dahn theer - an' tha wants to get rid of it, 'cause it doesn't half bloody stink!" Skegness camp was the first venture by Billy Butlin into the new and uncharted waters of British holiday camps. It was considered to be a luxury camp but at prices working people could afford. Three meals a day and all the sports and games activities free of charge and the cost was 35 shillings a week (£1.75)

Chapter Six

I HAD MOVED OUT OF MRS BAKER'S. She was a lovely lady but was for some reason reluctant to give me a key to the front door. This on occasions restricted my social life a great deal. At one of our 'away' darts matches a particular landlord was happy to keep open after hours and some of the lads stayed until one o'clock in the morning. They boasted about all the fun they'd had but I couldn't stay with them as I knew Mrs Baker would be staying up to let me in.

I sometimes left a party long before the finish as I would have felt guilty keeping an old lady up late. Eventually I felt I just had to leave. I took a ground floor flat right on the promenade. The front windows had wonderful views of the sea and Filey Brigg, and in the distance at night the beam from the lighthouse at Flamborough head. I had a chat with Bill Tennick and he told me what he knew about the Sports Stadium. Once again Billy Butlin was to prove that he didn't do things by half.

The stadium would have raked seating so that everyone would have a clear view of the action in the ring. There would be two large dressing rooms with showers and toilets. Most important from my point of view they were bringing in experienced fighters to do exhibitions on the Friday night and in most cases a 'known' professional. One of the names that Bill read out, Johnny Halafihi from Tonga, was one of the hottest names in boxing at that time. I began to feel thrilled at the prospect and what a pleasure it would be to be in a ring and moving around with someone who knew what they were doing. Johnny was a light heavy and so I would be sparring with him. Harry a lightweight at 9st 7lbs was much too small and Ken around 18 stones was too big.

I had blown up a bit from welterweight at 10st 7lbs and was now in the eleven stone mark but more the size of Johnny Halafihi than the other two. I knew I had to get fit and lost no time in making a start. I began running almost every night right along the sea front, starting at the Cobble landing and finishing just below the White Lodge Hotel. Within a few weeks I was doing six of these comfortably and starting to feel good.

Bill sent for me a couple of weeks before the 'Get In' crew were due to arrive. He explained that it would be the departments responsibility to erect the ring and that was additional to the normal jobs. So he had made arrangements for me to go onto the entertainment departments pay roll to make a start on a few of the opening jobs. He explained that would involve putting up the tennis nets dart boards, table tennis nets and other such stuff. I was pleased to wash my paint brushes for the last time.

On reflection it had been a hard winter and the job hadn't been the most pleasant. But, I had achieved all I had set out to do and knew the staff and the managers, the camp and Butlins as a company far better than when I started. I was looking forward to the 'Get In' crew arriving and seeing their friendly faces. Patsy wouldn't be with them but would arrive with the main intake two weeks later. Patsy and I had exchanged letters but occasionally rather than frequently. Her letters were far more interesting than mine. She had done a modelling job here and a photo shoot there and I could only boast of painting thirty chairs, eight wardrobes and a bed.

I had stopped driving the lads to work and was now chauffeuring Bill, which was a good arrangement as the short journey enabled us to discuss jobs that had to be done before the 'Opening Crew' arrived. Suddenly the long awaited moment came - they would arrive tomorrow. Patsy wouldn't be with them but would join us with the main staff intake in two weeks time.

They started arriving in dribs-and-drabs throughout the day and it was great being able to welcome each one of them. I had been asked by Bill to tell them that a meeting had been called for 8.30 the following morning. The lads moved straight on camp and I moved with them. Cappy, the staff accommodation manager was an amiable sort of bloke and he agreed that Patsy and Harry could move back into their old chalets. I had got to know Cappy quite well during the winter as I had spent so much time with him on the staff camp. Having worked the winter was paying dividends in numerous directions. I went to draw my red and whites from the clothing store and Neville the man in charge kindly issued me with two brand new sets and I was delighted to see they were the new issue with blue braid.

I had noticed the previous season that one of the Redcoats, Gerry Maxim, had somehow managed to look immaculate. His blazer fitted perfectly and his trousers had been tapered to 16 inch bottoms. My own issue trousers had turn ups, which I hated, and 22 inch bottoms. When I quizzed Gerry he told me that if I paid the wardrobe mistress for the Revue Company a few bob and a box of chocolates she would alter my uniforms for me. I asked for the waist of the blazer to be taken in, the sleeves shortened and the trousers tapered to 16 inch bottoms!! I had bought a pair of naval officers white canvas tropical issue shoes and intended to look the cats whiskers.

I drove the lads to the Imperial that evening to celebrate our reunion after, what had been for me at least, a long uncomfortable winter. It took two trips both ways as there was eight of them. Bill and Marjory joined us and it was a pleasant get-together.

At our meeting the next morning Bill outlined the jobs that had to be done before the intake of the first Campers. A lot of work was needed by every department to get the camp ready to open. The tennis nets and the signs had to be installed around the tennis courts,. The putting and crazy golf flags had to go out. Basketball and netball post had to be put out and the pitches marked. Soccer goal posts had to be painted and later the goal nets put up. As the only driver on the team I was in demand as Johnny wanted to put the whole equipment on the back of a pick-up truck and drop it off with some of the lads a various points. Johnny and I painted the goal posts from the back of the pick-up rather than use a ladder and we would later put the nets up the same way. The pitches and the sports field were marked out in creosote and Johnny explained that this burned into the roots of the grass and it was only necessary to mark the lines once a season. I found that I was working with Johnny on a daily basis. We worked well together and came in on the same wavelength. I supervised the erection of the boxing ring which was no problem as I had done it many times in the forces. The last few days we worked until dusk and suddenly Johnny announced we were ready to open.

A couple of days later the staff started to arrive. Patsy had let me have her train times and Johnny gave me time off to pick her up at York.

It was wonderful seeing Patsy again and it was great to see the others too. We had the usual induction meeting which was so helpful to new staff and, if nothing else, a refresher for the rest. I was asked to show the new Redcoats around the camp which pleased me and I saw it as another step forward.

At a morning meeting Bill told us that Wilf Orange had become Butlins full time dance festival organiser and, from an office here at Filey, would now be arranging dance festivals on all the Butlin camps. He also informed us that a new entertainment manager would be arriving. His name was Marten Tiffen, who had been manager of the Butlin Ocean hotel at Brighton. He would be arriving by train at York and I would be picking him up at 2.30 tomorrow afternoon.

York was a busy station with, as a rule, lots of arrivals so to make recognition easier I took my Redcoat blazer to slip over my shoulders as the train pulled in.

I was soon approached by a well-dressed man smiling broadly and saying *"You must be Rocky?"* I smiled back saying *"And you must be Mr Tiffen!"* He continued *"I didn't expect a Redcoat guard of honour"* We both laughed as I was wearing a brand new Redcoat blazer over a pair of old working trousers and tatty trainers, both had been considerably splattered with creosote. He was a friendly, talkative man who I took an immediate liking to. He asked me about the preparations for the opening and I told him that both Bill Tennick and Johnny had confirmed that the department was ready. We talked about the new sports stadium and he said that was what it would be called 'The New Sports Stadium'.

He told me that it was the prototype for stadiums to be built on other camps and would be very much under the spotlight this season. He told me there would be morning and afternoon sessions of training and sparring. He confirmed what Bill had said about established boxers coming in for weekly exhibitions on Friday evenings and, of course, I already knew about the 'All Star Wrestling'. He said he would arrange a meeting with Johnny and myself to talk about things in more detail. He asked a bit about my boxing experience and seemed happy enough with what I told him although by this stage I had decided that he wouldn't be a boxing fan. He just wasn't that sort of man his demeanor was that of a gentle person.

His hands were pink and soft and his nails had been polished. He spoke with a refined and educated accent and was rather 'delicate' but without being feminine. I drove him down the lines to his chalet and off-loaded his luggage. He gave me a small leather suitcase, a briefcase and a number of cardboard tubes, which he asked me to drop off at his office. He asked me to wait at the office for him. He arrived shortly after me and started to open the cardboard tubes. They each contained a number of posters and there were eight in total. He asked me to put them on his office walls; indicating certain areas. When I opened them out I saw they were theatrical posters and I was most impressed. It became apparent that our Marten Tiffen, the new entertainment manager at Filey, was a former West End musical comedy star who had performed with some of the biggest names in the business. The first bill I pinned up showed him sharing top billing with the famous Hy Hazell, I had recently read that she was now starring in Espresso Bongo, at London's famous Saville theatre. He had starred in "Zip Goes a Million", one of the West Ends most successful musicals, also "Half a Sixpence", which had been huge, and "Blue For a Boy", another smash hit.

He'd also had top billing for "Charlie's Aunt" and, despite the part having been played by Nowel Coward, Rex Harrision and Danny La Rue, he was billed as "Marten Tiffen The Best Charlie's Aunt In The Business". Quite a remarkable man this 'delicate' Mr Tiffen.

Opening a camp was always a happy and exciting experience and that went for staff of every department, catering, accommodation, shops and bars, coffee bars and amusement park. Whatever the department, everyone was hustling and bustling and putting together the final touches before we opened the gates for the first guests of the season. Every time you turned a corner you bumped into a friend from last year.

Despite his long journey 'Tiff', as Marten quickly became known, called his first Redcoat show rehearsal that night at midnight and we all knew it would go on until 2.30 or 3.O'clock in the morning. After a hard day's work it could be pretty tiring but all the Redcoats enjoyed the rehearsals and they were great fun. With all the others I was put in the Opening and Finale and was delighted when Johnny, who did the comedy picked me out to be in a couple of sketches. I loved performing and had discovered the previous season that I seemed to have a certain bent for it. I had decided that entertaining wasn't much different from boxing, both demanded being in the spotlight and the centre of attention.

Marten produced the Opening and the Finale and a few of the girls came out on stage to demonstrate how we should march on in time to the music. I loved performing in the Redcoat show and rehearsed hard, even going over everything with Patsy in the chalet. I was like a dog with two tails when Johnny asked me to play Billy Bouncer in the Old Time Music Hall. I wore a bowler hat, crepe hair moustache, a bow tie and a waistcoat but without a shirt. Patsy managed to get me some black woollen ballet tights and I wore a pair of boxing boots. Patsy drew some tattoo's on me with an eye brow pencil. I did a couple of tired old gags with Johnny but they still got laughs. *"Mister Bouncer I've got a dog with no nose!"* I would reply *"You've got a dog with no nose Mr Chairman? But how does it smell?"* Johnny would answer *"Terrible Mister Bouncer - Ruddy terrible!"* Throughout the show he would order me to throw out members of the audience. Playing Chairman Johnny was his usual brilliant, funny self! He would say *'I've got a cat Mister Bouncer-I've got a cat!"* and I would ask *"What do you call your cat Mr Chairman"* Johnny would say *"Cooking Fat"* and I would ask *"Why do you call it Cooking Fat?"* Johnny would reply *"Every time I come home drunk I fall over it - and say 'I'll Kill That Cooking Fat!"*

The music hall was a superb Recoat bar show which was greatly enjoyed by the campers and was a wonderful opportunity for Redcoats to develop their talents. It was a good 'money spinner' for the bars department as the tills were rattling all night long. Martin had officially designated me as 'In Charge' of the boxing team and the stadium and had asked me to think of ways that we could extend its use beyond boxing and wrestling. He asked me to let him have a weekly report on attendances and anything else I thought might be relevant. After considering this I gave him a couple of suggestions. There was a section of the floor at one side of the ring that had been left level for training purposes such as skipping, floor exercises and shadow boxing. It was where we also did our basic instruction.

This flat area was about 30 feet square and I suggested to him that when a wet weather programme was required a trampoline could be brought in and, if we could obtain a large tarpaulin to protect the ring canvas, between the sessions of boxing we could run fun and games inside the ring. Marten liked the idea and said he would order a tarpaulin.

The New Sports Stadium got off to a very good start and was busy at every session throughout the week. I had put a programme together which Marten had approved. Although we had the odd few campers who only came to the session once and we never saw them again, the actual participants numbered about 30 at each session and they mostly became regulars. The crowd that gave us a total of 80 to 100 at each session was made up of parents or friends of those taking part. The training was split into three sections, in different areas, and Ken, Harry and I each took an area but swapped around quite often.. There would be the sparring in the ring and this was usually done by

Harry or me as Ken was too big for the majority of them. One of us would take the skipping, shadow boxing and floor exercises. Someone would take a class using the speed ball and the big bag and giving instruction. We had teenagers and young men wanting to put the gloves on and we always tried to cater for this. If they were average size then Harry or I would put the gloves on with them. If they were very big blokes then Ken would go in with them. We had lots of youngsters coming in with mum and dad and that's what Harry and I really enjoyed. We used to laugh at the way the young ones would avoid 'Big Ken' like the plague.

The group I enjoyed most were perhaps between ten and fifteen years old because you could actually teach that age group the basic principles. When you first let them put the gloves on they would always stand too upright and rigid, and you would explain that if someone threw a punch they couldn't sway back to avoid it. You would get them into a more crouched position and show them how they could now roll back so the punch fell short. You could show them how, if they were fighting an orthodox fighter with a left lead, it was better to circle to their left away from his punches. If they moved to the right they were moving onto them.

When they first faced you they would always do so very square on showing their opponent their full front. You would explain that this shortened their punches and you would point out if they faced an opponent more sideways on it lengthened their punch. All very basic stuff but adequate for a young kid just getting started. The place had been packed out for the 'All Star Professional Wrestling'. Tiff had confirmed that Johnny Halafihi would be with us on Friday for the exhibition in the evening and we had constantly plugged it throughout the week. Halafihi's name was Johnny but I will now call him John to avoid any confusion with Johnny O'Mahoney.

We had also been told that Billy Butlin and a few directors would also be in attendance. I asked Marten if Colonel Brown would be with them and he asked what I knew of Colonel Brown. I explained that he had been the President of the National Sporting club where I had fought a few times when the Colonel had usually presented the trophies and someone had told me he was also a director of Butlins. Marten confirmed that Colonel Brown would be with them. I had learned the previous season that he was Director of Entertainment and Billy Butlins right hand man.

Rocky with fellow Redcoat Brian Massey, French Bar Filey 1957, with a party of 'Happy Campers'.

House Captain Filey 1958, with happy, smiling campers.

Rocky, Boxing Instructor Filey 1957

Chapter Seven

IT WAS WRITTEN INTO JOHN'S CONTRACT that he would attend prize giving on Friday afternoon to present the prizes, there would be around 3,000 campers there and it was a great plug for the exhibition. I knew we were going to get a big crowd on the night. Johnny came to the stadium early in the afternoon and we were able to put the gloves on and work out a few things for the exhibition bout. We did this in the privacy of a dressing room as I didn't want to expose him to the large crowd of people at the training session. John had done lots of exhibition bouts in the past and taught me a couple of very clever and realistic looking moves. The cue for me to do this was when he threw three simultaneous, straight lefts. I then had to duck low and go in for his body hitting him round the ribs with open gloves. The blows were nothing more than slaps but the loud noise they produced was most convincing! This would never have been done in a real fight of course as it left my head wide open for a counter punch.

    I found him to be a really nice genuine bloke and there was nothing affected about him in any way. Marten had told me to take him to his managers table in the dining room and I arranged to do this although I couldn't stay with him as I had to get to the theatre for the Redcoat Show.

    The show was entitled "Happily Ever Laughter" and there two houses, 5.30 to 6.30 and 7.00 to 8.00, it was a rush but worked well as the exhibition was at 8.30pm. Tommy Cassidy would referee and Harry and his opponent would be the opening bout. Harry said he had found someone reasonable to spar with and Big Ken had also found someone with a bit of experience. I got to the stadium with plenty of time to prepare as Johnny and I were the last bout and both Ken and Harry were doing three x 3 minute rounds with one minute intermission.

    The stadium was packed and I closed a blind eye to people standing in the rear aisle. There was a tremendous buzz of excitement. It was all for John of course who had enjoyed a great deal of press coverage on the sports pages recently and was eighth contender for Archie Moore's world title.

    Harry's bout was underway and as I peered from behind the door I saw the Billy Butlin entourage arrive. He was with a party of five or six other smart suited men and they stood just inside the entrance looking round. I knew they must be pleased with what they saw. The place was packed and the atmosphere was electric. Harry's bout was going very well. He was a beautiful mover and a great little fighter and drawing almost continuous applause from the very enthusiastic crowd.

I turned to look at John and he was sitting on a bench with his eyes closed and his head tilted back, he had a sort of half smile on his face and I imagined that this would be his practice before any bout. Just relaxing and getting his head right. This was always the mark of a good fighter and something that I had learned to do. Some fighters couldn't learn the trick and, as a result, I saw more fights lost in a dressing room than ever in a boxing ring. There was tremendous applause at the end of Harry's bout and I glanced towards the entourage and was delighted to see that they were all applauding too.

Ken and his opponent were in the ring and Tommy was giving them 'instructions'.

They were both big lads. Since giving up boxing Ken had made drinking beer a hobby and could quaff an enormous number of pints. At a guess I would say he was well over 18 stones. His opponent was a big lad too so I knew the audience would love this as fight fans like to see the big lads having a go. I watched the first round and it was very well received. I then joined Johnny who had started warming up. Ken's bout ended well and I glanced again at the directors with Billy Butlin who were applauding with almost as much enthusiasm as the campers. Tommy had suggested introducing John and me from the dressing room so the crowd could then follow John all the way to the ring. Tommy introduced me first of course *"Your senior boxing coach, former welterweight champion and Yorkshire's own Rocky Mason"* I was delighted with the applause and acknowledged it as I made my way to the ring.

One of the Redcoat seconds removed my dressing gown and I shadow boxed to entertain the crowd. I could hear Tommy on the microphone introducing John *"Ladies and Gentlemen, from Tonga the man who will shortly be fighting Yolande Pompey for the British and Empire light Heavy Weight title. Eighth contender for Archie Moore's world title .... Johnny Halafihi!!"*

What an ovation! They almost raised the roof I glanced across at the Butlin party and the Guv'nor was looking decidedly pleased. Tommy called us to the centre of the ring for his supposed instructions. We touched gloves and then I was moving round with a fighter I had no right to be in the ring with. He was suddenly gently popping my head back with hands so fast that I never saw them leave his body. Suddenly three simultaneous fast left jabs, it was my cue and I was under his last jab and slapping him very fast with open gloves. I danced away to a cheer from the crowd. It must have looked great to them seeing one of their Redcoats giving it round the belly to the eighth contender for a world title. John was one enormously talented fighter, gentle and generous with me to a fault. What an exhibition and the crowd absolutely loved it. I knew Billy and his party must be well pleased. I was happy also for Marten Tiffen, who was a nice man and we hadn't let him down. Harry was in the dressing room waiting and said *"That was brilliant mate, you had them up on their bleedin' toes tonight!!"*

We had showered and I was back in my red and whites ready to go to the ballroom when Marten came into the dressing room. He thanked us all for, in his words, a splendid show and told John and me that Mr Butlin and his party were delighted and they would like us to join them for a drink. I had been rushing to get to the ballroom and was dressed and ready but John had just finished his shower. Tiff said he would see us in the Harvey Bar and left. I waited a few minutes for John to dress and pack his gear and then we strolled over to the bar.

I had seen Colonel Brown with the party of directors because he was so easily recognised, as he was the only man outside of films that I had seen using a monocle, which he wore on a gold chain around his neck. He had the manner and bearing of a true gentleman and had always said a few kind words whenever he had presented me with a trophy.

Marten came over as we entered the bar and after getting a drink for us he started to introduce us to the various directors. I saw that Billy Butlin and the Colonel were engrossed in conversation together at the far end of the bar. Everyone was complimentary and especially to John of course the real star of the show.

Marten introduced us first to Billy Butlin and then he introduced John to the Colonel. The Colonel had a brief conversation with John before turning to me and putting a hand on my shoulder, saying *"I have met Rocky on several occasions when he boxed at the National sporting club of which I am a member.* I noticed that he didn't boast by saying *"I am the president"*. He continued *"You have done an excellent job in the new stadium Rocky, and it's nice to have you on board."* He struck up a conversation between John and myself and seemed to know quite a bit about John's record and history. He asked me a few questions about the stadium and I told him about the wet weather programme and our usual attendance numbers. He seemed genuinely interested in chatting with us and we didn't get the 'bums rush' I had half expected. Billy himself occasionally joined in to ask the odd question and I was surprised at his accent. He had a rather high pitched voice and what I took at first to be a rather strange American accent but would later learn was a mixture of South African and Canadian.

The following morning Marten asked me to his office where, after again thanking me for a successful opening week in the stadium and the excellent exhibitions, he told me about a conversation he'd had with Colonel Brown. He said that everyone had been so impressed with the exhibition and the atmosphere it had created in the New Sports Stadium that, despite the high cost involved, Mr Butlin wanted a second exhibition on another night of the week. Tiff wanted to know what night I felt it should be presented. I asked him if I could go away and think about it and he agreed. He asked me to go back to him that afternoon as he wanted to give the Colonel an answer that day.

I went off to quietly give the matter a bit of serious thought. We had the wrestling on Wednesday evening and so that left Monday, and Tuesday as I wouldn't want another exhibition on Thursday, the night before the main one.

I realised that bringing in a boxer of the calibre of John Halafihi wouldn't come cheap also of course travel expenses would be involved. I suddenly got an idea, the person doing an exhibition didn't really have to be a 'name', we had that on Friday with John Halafihi. All that was required was an experienced boxer who was capable of demonstrating good boxing skills. Why not engage another instructor? We were cheap enough and another advantage was that we would also have his services throughout the week. If we booked a welter or light - welterweight Harry could do an evening exhibition with him on Monday and I could go in with him on Tuesday afternoon. Another idea came to me. Why confine the trampoline sessions to the wet weather programme? There was plenty of time to use a trampoline between our sessions and a bit of trampoline instruction would compliment the new stadium building. I met with Marten and told him my ideas on the exhibition also that we could have sessions on the trampoline each day at 9.00am until 10.00 and 5.00 until 6.00. Before and after the boxing sessions and doing this would also increase the use of the stadium. I could see that Marten was impressed and Johnny later confirmed this by telling me that Marten had phoned the printer to have the trampoline sessions included in the programme without delay.

Marten had totally accepted my proposal about the boxing and was going to put it to the Colonel.

A few days later he sent for me to say that Colonel Brown had agreed and he asked me to contact someone suitable to bring in as a coach and to do the extra exhibitions. I suddenly realised that I didn't know anyone and went looking for Harry. I knew Harry was a good bet as he was so well known in boxing circles around London. He occasionally trained fighters for the legendary Al Phillips "The Aldate Tiger". Harry was also a licenced referee and second and, just as I knew he would, he came up trumps and promised to phone around. He spent that evening making calls from Johnny's office phone. A boxer that Harry eventually found was well known to him and had all the right credentials.

His name was Eddie West, a former welterweight with a lot of experience. He had well over 100 fights under his belt and had a good win record. He was out of work and anxious to start as soon as possible. Marten said he could travel here and sign his contract on arrival. This was good news for everyone and I made arrangements, through Harry, to pick Eddie up at York the following day. The reason it was better to collect people from York was that everyone left the train there and there was an hours wait for a connection to Filey.

I liked Eddie West at first sight. He was a good looking lad, smartly dressed and in his mid-twenties. He was a chatterbox and in what seemed no time at all we were driving through the camp gates. We went to the office where we were met by Johnny who took him in to see Tiff to sign his contract . I parked the car and went to relieve Harry so he could spend a bit of time with Eddie.

Eddie settled in immediately and the next day we put the gloves on and had a move around together. He was a clever, experienced boxer, a nice mover with fast hands and very fit. I think we all knew that Eddie was surplus to requirements and had been taken on to save money doing exhibitions. I began to think that in a week or two, when everything had settled down, I might be able to work that to my advantage! He was a smart dresser and I tipped him off that he could get his uniform altered to fit him better if he 'made love' to the Gaiety Theatre wardrobe mistress!!

That night I was on theatre duty in the Gaiety for the second show and watched one of the lads doing a warm-up. I knew if given the chance I could do it. Some of the Redcoats were better than others and this lad was very nervous. I would say that over the years I had spent more time in front of an audience than most of them, for very different reasons of course, but it was still performing to an audience. I had formed the impression that there was something of a pecking order amongst the Redcoats and it did seem that those who had done a few seasons had a bit of priority over newer Red's. Bingo Betty did a nice warm-up and she was excellent on the microphone. I also liked her personality when doing 'Goodnight Campers'. I'd been watching things closely and I felt confident that when my turn came I could do it.

Whenever I left a theatre duty I would go to the ballroom via the Sportsmans or Gaiety Bar and spend five minutes watching the entertainers. On a groups night off it might be Johnny and Ronnie with the young Redcoat on guitar who, I had learned was Russ Hamilton. Russ was a children's entertainer who joined the two boys when he had closed the children's theatre. I would watch the audience reaction to something the lads did and would have loved to be a part of it. All I needed was the right opportunity and that was coming sooner than I expected!

I was chatting with Julie Rolls, the singer and Ernie, who was Teddy Fosters keyboard player, Ernie told me about a routine that he had played for on an American army base. He said it went down very well and he explained it in detail. I thought it was tremendous and Ernie said he would be happy to rehearse it with me and I just couldn't wait. I later wrote down a couple of running-orders and gave one to Ernie, which he approved and we arranged to rehearse it in the theatre with no one else about. I certainly didn't have one of the best voices around but that wasn't needed and I could at least sing in tune. Ernie quickly found my key and ran through the routine with me three or four times. By then I felt totally confident and couldn't wait to do it. It was a party dance routine that I knew would go down well in the Viennese Ballroom. I spoke to Johnny who told me to do it during 'Party Dances'.

That night I was almost quivering with excitement. Ernie had prepared Teddy who had also played for the routine. I briefed a few of the Redcoats about what was happening. Then went on stage and took the microphone and, with a cymbal clash from the drummer started the patter. *"Ok, everyone join in behind the Redcoats and we want you in one long*

Conga line all the way around the room". The band played the Conga and the Redcoats started to lead the long line around the floor. I gave the drummer a nod and he gave the cymbals a resounding crash and the band stopped playing.... *"OK, we are not going to do the Conga. We are going to put you aboard a train and take you to all four corners of the world. Everybody Get aboard The Train!!* The band now played 'California' and the Redcoats took the train all-round the ballroom floor. I would stop the train in various countries and the Campers would do the tradional dance of that country. France the Can-Can, Ireland the Irish Jig, America the Jive. It was something new and everybody loved it. It seemed to open a door for me and Teddy asked me to do some square dance calling. I bought a piano copy of Soloman Levy and it became a regular routine. Johnny knew I had a great desire to be involved and started using me a bit more often. It wasn't long before I was doing warm-ups in the theatre.

Johnny, Ronnie, Pat and I were going over to Skegness the following week and I decided to get to the theatre early to see the warm-up. It might just give me a few new ideas. I was doing the party dances and square dancing on a couple of nights a week now and Johnny was detailing me for the warm-ups on a weekly basis. I felt that I was getting more experience all the time and I had certainly realised there was no substitute for actually getting up and doing it.

The Old Time Music Hall was going from strength to strength and Johnny and I were also getting good laughs in the Redcoat show. Johnny, Ronnie, with Patsy and myself had formed a friendship and we would often get together for a late night drink. Our trips to Skegness were something we all looked forward to and had become a laugh a minute.

Billy Butlin and the Colonel visited occasionally and always looked in on the stadium. They had complimented Marten on the trampoline sessions. Which had become busier than we had expected and kept the stadium in use right throughout the day.

Every camp had a chief hostess whose job it was to allocate prizes for the winners of competitions and events. Our hostess was an attractive girl called Maggie Lamond who had been with the Company for quite a few years.

Apart from being hostess at Filey, Maggie was also the Butlin Chief Hostess and worked at the Head Office in London during the winter. Patsy had come back this season as Maggie's assistant and they had become good friends. Maggie would often join our late night drinking sessions with Johnny and Ronnie and occasionally she would drop into our chalet to have a nightcap with us. Maggie was a long standing 'partner' of Wally Goodman, Colonel Brown's assistant. On the odd occasion the three of us had driven a mile or so up the road to the Reighton Country Club, where the Teddy Foster band were staying. Maggie, Patsy and Julie had become friendly and we would join Julie and Teddy to relax over a couple of drinks. One evening Patsy and I went up alone and found a table with Teddy and Julie. After a few minutes Maggie arrived in the company of Wally and Marten Tiffen. I felt a bit uncomfortable at first but we were soon to be put at our ease and I began to realise, when off duty, just what good fun Wally and Marten were.

'Lofty' Herman, the former England and Hampshire cricketer was cricket coach at Filey, and the former Pompey footballer Phil Gunter was the soccer coach. Johnny came up with an idea of running a 'Sportsman's Quiz'. He would be the question master and he asked Ronnie and me if we would join Lofty and Phil on the panel. My sports knowledge was pretty much confined to boxing, Ronnie was a good all-rounder and Phil and Lofty knew their sports pretty well. It was good entertainment and was well received by the campers.

Sadly the end of season seemed to be approaching all too quickly. But I was quite pleased, looking back over the weeks, at how much I had learned. I was singing and doing comedy in the Music Hall, I felt comfortable in the Opening and Finale of the Redcoat Show and was getting laughs with Johnny in the sketches. Doing the train routine was a nightly event and I'd learned a couple more square dances. I had become really good mates with Johnny and Ronnie and we'd had a good few laughs together. I had thought about it, and I was growing to love the job more and more as time went by, but I couldn't even think about staying on the camp again this winter. It was looking as if I would be going home for a few months. Eddie had really settled in well, he was a sensible bloke and would have no trouble running the stadium next season.

We had discussed it and he was really keen. I had intended to approach Marten about doing GDs next year, but out of the blue he sent for me. He said he liked the way I had got the new stadium venture started, and I knew he had been talking to Johnny when he said that now it was up and running it could handed over to someone else next season. He asked me what I thought my future in the company might be. Which gave me an opportunity to tell him how much I enjoyed being with Butlins and wanted it to be my way of life. I told him that I felt I had something to offer Butlins and it was much more than just running a sports stadium.

We had an interesting chat and I felt it was rewarding. He sent for me again a couple of days later. When I left is office after a few short minutes my mind was in a whirl. I couldn't believe what I'd heard and I just had to find Patsy to tell her. I was going on the Redcoat team at Brighton for the winter!! I just couldn't believe it, to be retained was every Redcoats dream., and I was finding it almost impossible to take in - it was beyond my own wildest dreams. Ronnie was coming too but Johnny had declined as he wanted time with his family in Ireland.

Chapter Eight

EVERYONE WAS PAID AN END OF SEASON BONUS which usually amounted to the equivalent of a week's wages. The Company was still recovering from a failed venture in the Bahamas. Billy Butlin had tried unsuccessfully to launch a camp there and a great deal of money had been lost. Perhaps as a result of this we were offered our bonus in cash or double the amount in Butlin shares. Like most of the others I knew I opted for the cash. Years later discussing this with Colonel Brown I was informed that if I had taken the shares, with free issues and bonuses over the years they would have been worth many thousands of pounds.

On a visit to the Bahamas in 1946 Billy Butlin thought he saw lots of potential for development. He purchased 700 acres at West End, the nearest point of the Bahamas to the Florida mainland on Grand Bahama. To give a comparison Butlins Filey, the largest holiday camp in the world, stands in 400 acres. He also bought two hotels, the Fort Montagu Beach in Nassau and the Princess in Bermuda, at that time the island was almost totally undeveloped. There was a shortage of both building materials and labour on the island and these had to be shipped in. Billy formed a public company incorporated in the Bahamas and was supported by several large British companies. Shares to the extent of some £2 million were issued. (£61 million at today's value.)

To further increase the costs, expatriate construction staff were moved in, necessitating the building of temporary accommodation. Due to the dock strike in Great Britain, which lasted over three months, materials and supplies were held up, seriously impeding the progress of building and again adding further to the cost. Eventually after many long delays and setbacks the holiday village was opened in February 1950. However, mainly due to the inflated cost of construction the project was not paying its way and was closed down.

Johnny and a few of the others were staying on for a few days to close the department down. Just as there was an 'opening team' to put the nets and equipment out at the start of a season. There was a 'close down' team to put the things away. I wanted to travel to Brighton with Ronnie but as he lived nearby in Newcastle he was having a couple of days with his family before travelling. Patsy and I went as far as London together.

Butlins Ocean Hotel Brighton, was actually in Saltdean some

six miles or so out of town. I suppose giving the address as Brighton was sensible as everyone had heard of Brighton and it immediately conjured up a seaside image. On the other hand who had heard of Saltdean? The hotel was designed like an ocean liner and had many of the features you would find on a ship, these included brass framed circular portholes in and around reception. It was constructed in 1937 and occupied a site of four acres with 344 bedrooms. During the Second World War the hotel became one of the main Auxiliary Fire Stations on the south coast and was later a fire service college.

Everyone had an image of Billy Butlin, as the jovial, smiling, charitable champion of the working classes, and he was all of that. But he was also a very astute businessman with a showman's fairground guile. The Company bought the Ocean Hotel in 1953, but Billy Butlins first offer was flatly refused. There was no way the esteemed residents of Saltdean would tolerate *anything* Butlins in the area.

The local watering hole is The Spanish Lady, a delightful pub 150 yards down the road from The Ocean. Wally Goodman dropped in for a gin and tonic on a couple of occasions. Wally has what could be described as a rather impressive military bearing, helped by his white hair and a full waxed moustache. Syd' the landlord welcomed Wally *"Good evening Sir. I don't think we've seen you around these parts. New are you?"* Wally responded *"Yes, I'm new to the area but you'll be seeing a lot more of me. I am the Governor of the new open prison up the road at the Ocean."* Over the next few days a number of strange men and women in navy blue uniforms began appearing in the hotel grounds taking measurements and photographs. Rumours spread around the area like a rampant forest fire. Wally dropped in for another gin and tonic and was happy to confirm the rumours. Billy made a second offer and was welcomed with open arms!

Billy Butlin often said that The Ocean Hotel was one of the best investments he ever made. Situated, as it was, just above the beautiful Saltdean cliffs and just a short drive or bus ride from the lovely town of Brighton. Being so near London we naturally drew a lot of bookings from London and the greater London area. The hotel was packed with guests throughout the summer and if you wanted to book for Christmas you had to book before August or you couldn't get in. The place was also packed to the doors for the Reunion Weekends as special rates were offered to guests throughout the summer to return for a fun packed weekend during the winter. A team of Redcoats was sent to London's Victoria station on Fridays and coaches were laid on to bring them from Brighton station. Just after Christmas until March the hotel became a honeymooner's paradise. In those days if young people got married before a certain date in March they got a full year's tax rebate and the hotel was packed to the doors with newlyweds. This gave the Redcoats a chance for a weekly laugh. Head office had arranged for every couple to be given a souvenir gift which just happened to be an alarm clock. These were presented in a packed ballroom at 8.o'clock on Sunday evening. Three or four of us had spent half an hour setting all the alarms to go off at ten minutes past eight!!

Most of the male Redcoats were accommodated in a house about 200 yards from the hotel, it was a delightful old Tudor-style place called High Lodge. It had black solid timber facings dressing the white exterior walls and was big, detached and had large split level gardens. It had been the home of a Butlin director when the company first acquired the hotel.

Brett Cresswell was the entertainment manager, Freddy Gordon the bandleader and the department was staffed by an assortment of Redcoats from a number of the camps. Wally Piggot was a comedian and had been the compere at Pwllheli. Keith Ellam was another comic who had been compere at Ayr. They formed a double act during the forthcoming winter calling themselves Pearl & Dean, until the advertising company of the same name threatened legal action and they became Lester and Smart. Jack Marshall was a talented key board player and, until he moved to Clacton, we had been at Filey together the previous year. Lynda Noone had spent the summer at Brighton and was a dancer. Jimmy Noone, Lynda's husband, was the resident organist. Shirley Denton was an excellent Redcoat from Skegness. Brian Mathews was also a first-class Redcoat from Clacton.

Peter Millington, who was permanent at Brighton, was a very talented musician who played keyboard, trumpet and trombone. Ronnie and I were from Filey, of course. Mair Davis was a lovely Welsh vocalist from Pwllheli. Ron Stanway was a GD Redcoat who in years to come would become General Manager of Entertainments. In the 1950s there were six camps with Bognor, Barry and Minehead yet to be built. It's a fairly educated guess that the Redcoats on each camp at that time averaged sixty and that gave a total of 360 on all the camps. If Margate had the same number of Redcoats as Brighton that meant a total of only 24 had been retained for the winter and I began to wonder what could be so special about my new colleagues at Brighton, for them to have been kept on over the winter?. Over the next few months I was most certainly going to find out!!

    I have always felt that at Butlins a great deal can be learnt from your peers. In my two seasons at Filey I felt that I had learned so much by watching Johnny, Ronnie, Bingo Betty and others. I would realise very soon that I had been given an opportunity to now watch and learn from the crème-de-le-crème!

    I was soon to discover that by just watching them going naturally about their duties this body of young people were the very epitome of what a Redcoat should be and the absolute personification of what real Redcoating was all about. It hadn't taken me long at Filey to realise that there was a deal of difference between the quality of general duty Redcoats. Quite a number of them were very good and a credit to their red and whites whilst others, and I would discover it was so on all the camps, were an absolute disgrace and shouldn't have even been in a red blazer.

    I have to say it was mainly some of the male Redcoats who smeared the true image of a Butlin Redcoat. Some of the lads, when realising the esteem in which the Redcoats were held by the guests, regarded the uniform as nothing more than a passport to crumpet. They couldn't see that wearing the uniform was an immense honour and a privilege. They simply saw it as a means of screwing around and getting a shag for the night. A side effect of this and their late night chalet parties was their frequent lateness for breakfast and their Redcoat duties. They might get away with it for a couple of seasons but they would eventually be found out.

    The following season they would be surprised and disappointed at not getting an invitation to return. They would stick in a mundane, boring job for a couple of years and then wake up to the fact that they'd had the greatest, most wonderful job in the world and had blown it. Today they would argue that fact and even deny it, but I am sorry lads in my 30 years with Butlins I saw you come and go and other honest Butlin people would have to say the same!

    Despite Ronnie trying to re-assure me I still felt a bit timorous at my first rehearsal watching, the others doing their spots as they all seemed so competent and professional. I had spoken to Johnny during our short time left together at Filey and, in answer to my question, he had confirmed that it was better for a Redcoat at the Ocean to have some sort of spot. He pointed out that I wouldn't be valued for doing any boxing instruction as they didn't have any. He had advised me to join in as many of the sing-songs as I could, get a part in the Old Time Music Hall and be seen on a microphone as often as possible. I had spent some weeks, just before leaving Filey trying to pluck up the courage to do a monologue and I was cursing myself now for not doing it.

I had however learned it by heart and thank goodness I had gone to Ernie with it as it required some background music not any particular tune to the number but just quiet background music which Ernie had called 'Hearts and Flowers'. Ernie played it solo on the organ but the entire orchestra sat there listening and when I finished they had all applauded. This rehearsal would in truth be the first time I had ever performed it in public and God forbid, I would be doing it in front of the best Redcoats who worked for Butlins. I was feeling more nervous than I ever felt stepping into a boxing ring.

It was a number I had heard on Radio Luxemburg and had been a big hit in America. It was later done by Max Bygraves and became a hit number for him too. It was now called 'A Deck of Cards' but had originally been called 'The Soldiers Almanac, Bible and Prayer Book'. It was a religious tale of an American soldier arrested for playing cards in church. It was set in World War ll, when a group of soldiers had gone to church.

While Scripture is being read, one man who has only a deck of cards pulls them out and spreads them out in front of him. He is immediately spotted by a sergeant, who believes the soldier is playing cards in church and orders him to put them away. The soldier is then arrested and taken before the Provost Marshall to be punished. The Provost Marshall demands an explanation. The soldier tells him that he didn't have a bible and explains to him the significance of each card.
I picked up the microphone, took three deep breaths and just went for it

When I see the Ace: it tells me there is but one God in heaven.
The Deuce: tells me the bible is split into two parts, The Old and the
New Testaments
The Three: is The Father, the Son and the Holy Ghost.
The Four: is the four evangelists who went out to preach the gospel- Mathew, Mark, Luke and John.

The Five: is the five virgins our lord saved, five were wise and were saved five were foolish and cast out.
The Six: tells me that in six days God made this heaven and earth.
The Seven: tells me that on the seventh day God rested from this great work
The Eight: reminds me of the eight people our Lord save during the floods there was Noah and his wife, their sons and their wives.
The Nine: is the nine lepers our lord cleansed. Nine out of ten didn't even thank him.
The Ten: is the Ten Commandments our Lord handed to Moses on a tablet of stone.
The Jack: or Knave is the Devil.
The King: is our Lord God almighty, king of this great heaven and earth.
There are 365 spots: equal to the number of days in a year.
There are 52 cards: equal to the number of weeks.
There are four suits: equal to the number of seasons.
There are twelve picture cards: equal to the number of months in a year.
So you see sir, my deck of cards serves me as a bible, prayer book and an almanac.

I couldn't believe my ears when Brett Announced *"That will be the Finale of our Redcoat Show."*

I was over the moon and started, at last, to feel part of the team. The following day at rehearsal Brett, who had obviously given some considerable thought to the matter told me to use the microphone at the front of the stage and he put the Redcoats on a rostrum behind me with the Freddie Gordon trio accompanying us and, as I started to speak the lines, the Redcoats began to quietly sing 'Glory, Glory, Hallelujah'.

Mine eyes have seen the glory of the coming of the Lord;
He is trampling out the vintage where the grapes of wrath are stored;
He hath loosed the fateful lightening of his terrible swift sword;
His truth is marching on.
Glory! Glory! Hallelujah! Glory! Glory! Hallelujah
Glory! Glory! Hallelujah! His truth is marching on.

I rehearsed it in my head so much, just going over it time after time, that I am sure I could have almost done it backwards. Halfway through the piece on the night of the show I became aware that you could have heard the proverbial pin drop and at the end I was almost stunned by the applause. Brett and the Redcoats were delighted and I realised myself that it was a most unusual, but very emotional end to the show.

Most Redcoats I had come across at Filey had been exuberant characters with some measure of personality and I supposed that's what made them apply for the job in the first place. But the Redcoats I was getting to know at Brighton were a different breed altogether, seeming to radiate charisma and positively bubbling with personality. The Redcoat Show produced by Brett was an absolute dream. I wasn't in any of the comedy sketches or scena's and just did the Opening and Finale, which gave me an opportunity to watch the others working from the wings. They were all first class, with Keith and Wally closing the show with 20 minutes of very funny comedy.

In 1955 Billy Butlin on a trip to America shared a seat with the famous film star Marlene Deitrich and couldn't believe this glamorous lady was a grandmother. On his return he asked Colonel Brown to incorporate the Glamorous Grandmother into the entertainment programme at all the camps and hotels, stressing that the accent must be on glamour. The weekly winners took part in a Southern or Northern Area Final, which culminated in 20 of them competing in a televised Grand final. Usually at the Ocean hotel. Another major Butlin competition was the 'National Holiday Princess', which was a weekly bathing beauty competition run on the same lines. The 'Miss She' was a fashion contest in 'Day Wear' and sponsored by the National Magazine company who published 'The She' magazine. It was run very much the same as the others.

After a few weeks I learned that I would be seeing Marten Tiffin much sooner than I had thought. At one of the morning meetings Brett informed us that we were presenting the Grand Final of the Holiday Princess in a couple of weeks and Marten, as the Butlin senior compere would be coming to present it. The event, Brett told us, would be covered by Southern Television. I had no idea that Marten was the company's senior compere but it didn't really surprise me, knowing of his experience in West End shows.

Wally and Keith were both experienced comperes and, after watching them on an assortment of competitions, I really admired their style. I presumed that as they were comperes they would do the bulk of the competitions and whatever event required the use of a microphone. I was surprised but very pleasantly pleased to see my name appear on a detail to compere the weekly Miss She fashion contest. It didn't worry me at all as I had done a couple of junior competitions at Filey and had watched our compere Maurice do the Miss She on a few occasions. I would find in ensuing weeks that it was Brett's policy to share the events between us and everyone got a chance. There was an enormous variety of things to do on a microphone from calling bingo, an assortment of competitions, quiz shows, the swimming gala, sing-songs and cabaret in the bar, party dances, square dancing. And all of it marvellous experience and an opportunity to compare your own performance against that of someone else.

Keith worked down on the floor when doing competitions in the ballroom but Wally worked on the stage. He would move from one side of the stage to the other, when making his opening remarks, talking to one section of the audience and then the other. I was standing with Brett on one show and he remarked *"I like the way he dresses the stage!"* That told me something and was just another little tit-bit I had learned. When I got the chance I tried doing it both ways and preferred to be on stage. I began to address one section of the audience and then move, still speaking, across the stage to now speak to another and I now knew that I was 'dressing the stage'. I had learned a lot from watching Keith and Wally and I knew it was a learning curve that would continue as the weeks went by.

I learned from the girls too and noticed when on reception duties the girls didn't just stand around 'dressing' the area but went forward to greet the guests as they came through the doors. They did it with convincing smiles and were so warm and friendly. They never missed an opportunity to chat with the guests and seemed to quickly get to know their names. When on sessions of bingo and working on the floor amongst the players as soon as a 'house' was called and the winner went to collect their prize it was an opportunity for them to approach different families or groups for a bit of friendly banter. Outside the dining rooms and during the 'Swanning' was another example of their friendly approach to the customer. I began to copy them as you didn't have much of a choice really and if you didn't act like them you would have been seen as some sort of outsider.

Brett asked me at a meeting if I had done any painting and I said that I had. He showed me a competition backdrop in the basement and said he would like it freshened up for the forthcoming competition finals. He explained that presentation was important as the event would be televised and that Colonel Brown and a few of the top brass would be visiting. Brett had shown me a lot of kindness and this was a small way I could repay him so I explained that painting this rather tatty backdrop wouldn't improve it very much and I could do a much better job by wallpapering it. Brett wasn't a very practical bloke and probably hadn't ever put a brush in a pot of paint in his life. He said he would leave it to me. I obtained a maroon paper with a gold Fleur De Lys design and when I had finished it did look most professional. The ballroom stage was about two feet high and the edge had become chipped and scratched. I explained to Brett that it could be greatly improved if I repainted it in black and then fixed white painted trellis to it.

Brett was delighted and gave me a free hand. When I had finished I put the set together and he was absolutely delighted and I must say I was pleased with the result myself. He asked if I could do something similar for the other two finals and I said that I would be happy to. I realised that I had probably also 'volunteered' for painting panto scenery and other bits but I didn't mind doing it and it seemed to please Brett and he'd been kind to me so why not?

We were told that Marten would arrive on Friday evening to start rehearsing the finalists on Saturday morning. Brett knew I worked for Marten and asked if I would like to help out organizing the girls. I was delighted as it was something I wanted to be involved in. I had learned that Tiff had been the compere at the Ocean and had taken over as manager the year before he came to Filey. Brett gave me a couple of hours with Marten when he arrived and over a drink we talked about what he wanted done for the show. It was wonderful to see him again and he seemed pleased that I was enjoying the Ocean. I made an early start the next morning as I wanted to have the set up before the television crew arrived. Marten had said they might want to do a bit of filming during rehearsals. The girls would be using a 'walkout' which was the same height as the stage, to take them out over the ballroom floor to where the judges would be seated I had painted this as well and fixed white trellis to the sides. I put the set up and was invited to join Brett and Marten for breakfast.

The rehearsals went smoothly with the hostess Lynda backstage organizing the girls and so I was free to be out front and able to watch Marten's performance. The TV cameras and lighting only added to the excitement and the atmosphere was electric. It was the first time I'd hear Tiff on a microphone and I marvelled at his splendid microphone voice and technique. Of course his many years in the West End had taught him that. He had a wonderful stage presence and presented the competition brilliantly. There was a formidable panel of judges which included Eamon Andrews, the famous broadcaster and presenter of 'This Is Your Life', Barbara Windsor, the star of the 'Carry On films', Frankie Howard, the comedian of radio and TV fame, Gareth Hunt, the well-known actor, and Gloria Huniford, the TV celebrity. Colonel Brown, his assistant Wally and Harold Vinter the Senior Press Officer had also joined us for the occasion. At the end of the competition they all retired for a few drinks before the special dinner that had been arranged. Brett, keen to fly the flag, had put eight of us on the late night sing-song which they looked in on at the end of the evening.

Marten had been superb and a few of us had stood almost open mouthed at his sheer professionalism. The Colonel, who had been a great fan of Tiff during his West End years, would much later tell me of Marten's sad fall from theatrical grace. It was decided to tour 'Zip Goes A Million' round the provinces and it seemed that Marten, who had starred for years in London theatres, was not accepted by the general northern public. In the West End of London, his cultured accent and urbane presence was adored, but they hated it in Bradford, Sheffield and Barnsley. Tiff was replaced by George Formby who was an instant success and that, as far as theatrical agents and producers were concerned, was the end of Marten Tiffen.

Marten would visit twice more when the whole thing would be repeated for the Miss She and Glamorous Grandmother finals, which he also presented superbly. I was happy to be a part of it even though it only involved painting and wallpapering the sets.

As Christmas was approaching I was again asked to accompany Brett to the junk room in the basement to find suitable bits of scenery that could be adapted for the pantomime. Brett told me it would be 'Aladdin And His Wonderful Lamp'. He had written the script which we went through together and it was decided that most scenes could be worked 'front cloth', which meant in front of the 'tabs' (Curtains) Only two scenes would be required 'Widow Twankey's Laundry' and 'The Palace'. I found a couple of flats that could easily become the laundry and I could convert the competition set into 'The Palace'.
Brett called the first rehearsal and passed around the script and there were yells of delight from those involved.

ALADDIN ……………….. The hero……….. ……. Lynda
ABANAZER…………….. The wicked uncle…… Wally
WISHEE WASHEE …….. Aladdin's brother…… Shirley
WIDOW TWANKEY…… The fearsome mother…. .Keith
TWO POLICEMEN……… Pep-Si & Ko-La………. Peter & Jimmy
EMPEROR OF CHINA…. A Buffoon…………… Ronnie
PRINCESS JASMINE…… Aladdin's love interest… Mair
GENIE OF THE LAMP… Not the brightest…… Ron

Stage Manager Rocky.
Spotlights Jack & Brian.

I wasn't too disappointed, although I would have liked a part but the others, with the exception of Mair, had all worked the Ocean before. They told us the panto' was the highlight of Christmas. It took all of us a week to put up the tree and decorations and then it was upon us!

Everyone had been right and what a marvellous Christmas it was. Most of the guests were regulars who came every year and before they left put their names down for the next one. There was a Christmas Punch Party, with the punch served in miniature glasses with handles, which were an imitation of a pint beer mug, and after the party you kept your glass as a souvenir. The enormous Christmas pudding was carried, flaming, around the dining room by Redcoats and Chef's in tall white hats. The Salvation Army came to sing carols. Santa gave every child a present on Christmas morning. The meals were excellent with free wine on every table for Christmas dinner. There were cabaret shows in the bar and the Redcoat Show and Pantomime on stage in the ballroom. The sing-songs continued until two in the morning. At the end of it we were all exhausted but wouldn't have missed it for anything.

Brett had used an imitation tree and wanted to store it and the baubles in a space above the dressing room. I offered to clear out boxes of rubbish to make room for this. I looked in one box and it was full of old running orders, memos and a few old contracts.

One in particular was dated 1956 and was for Bruce Forsyth for a Sunday Variety show it was for £12,00 and like an idiot I binned it. Easter was soon upon us and, like Christmas, the hotel was packed to the doors. Once again full of regulars and before the end of their stay they put down a deposit to book again for the following year.

I had started doing a nine minute singing spot in the Regency Bar, Brett had offered me twelve minutes but I only felt confident in three numbers. I had told Keith and Wally that I would love to do some comedy and on their advice I started doing the odd gag between numbers. I didn't have a very good voice and pretty soon the jokes were going down better than the songs. I was soon able to drop the vocals all together and go on as a 12 minute comedy spot I would have preferred 30 minutes but that was all Brett could allow. I felt more comfortable doing this and I was getting more confident as the weeks went by.

The Ocean was a wonderful place to be for the winter, the climate was very mild and the locals rarely saw any snow at all. There were some lovely coastal walks on a day off. Rottingdean, Peacehaven, and if you were feeling really energetic Newhaven Wharf. Brighton was a good town for shopping and I enjoyed wandering down 'The Lanes'.

I had enjoyed a fantastic time at Brighton and I had learned so much throughout the winter and it felt great putting it together in readiness for my return to Filey.

Chapter Nine

IT WAS WONDERFUL BEING BACK AT FILEY and seeing Patsy and the old team again. It was a fantastic feeling to be thrown into the melee that was the ritual of opening a holiday camp, midnight rehearsals, Redcoat meetings, induction and everything else that went with it. But most of all it was marvellous doing it as a general duty Redcoat The majority of last year's team were back and there were only eight new Redcoats. We managed to get in three midnight rehearsals for the Redcoat show, which was a tremendous plus as we would need only one final dress rehearsal in the hectic throes of the opening week.

During my winter absence at Brighton, Eric Bennett, the camp controller had left and been replaced by Ted Young. The title camp controller would soon be changed to general manager. Ted Young called a meeting with Marten knew what it was about and asked me to attend.

At the meeting was Jim Batten, maintenance manager, Ted Molt, transport manager and Jim Warhurst, chief of security. When he first opened the meeting I was sure it was a send up but I soon realised that he was being serious. He told us that Billy Butlin had somehow been informed that an elephant, somewhere or other, had painted a picture and the painting had been sold for a considerable amount of money. We were the team selected to ensure that Filey's, Big Charlie did the same.

The painting would take place in the transport yard which was in a quiet part of the camp that explained Ted Molt's presence. Jim Batten would provide the paint, brushes and what else might be required. Jim Warhurst would provide security to keep the Campers at a distance. I would be there to give a Redcoat presence. We then had what developed into a most serious discussion. It was decided that we couldn't stretch Big Charlie's talents further than doing an abstract painting.

The painting would be done on an 8ft x 4ft sheet of plywood. Charlie's best 'work' could later be cut out of this large sheet to give us a picture in a more suitable size. It was agreed that primary colours in gloss would be the best for Big Charlie to use and the board could first be primed in undercoat. It was finally decided that Charlie would paint in blue, yellow and red, and the undercoat, which would be applied by

Jim Batten, would be blue. We agreed to meet in the transport yard at ten o'clock the following morning.

The weather couldn't have been better, it was a dry sunny day with a clear blue sky. Charlie and his keeper Ibrahim were waiting when we arrived and, after a brief discussion, it was decided to lean the board against the transport office wall and raise it off the ground by standing it on a couple of crates. Jim Batten had brought a few brushes in different sizes and we agreed that Charlie should start with a two and a half inch brush. Jim Warhurst, who, in the past two days had become an expert in elephant artistry, told us that Ibrahim should give the brush to Charlie as it would have his smell on it. Ted Molt dipped the brush into the yellow gloss and handed it to Ibrahim, who then put the brush into Charlie's trunk. The elephant immediately tossed the brush to the far side of the yard. Our elephant expert Jim advised us to use a bigger, heavier one and Ted chose a six inch brush, dipping it again into the yellow. Charlie flung that one further than the first.

Elephant Jim then told us that Charlie didn't have enough handle to hold and we should tape a brush onto a broom handle. Ibrahim wanted to water the elephant and so we agreed to a break for lunch and meet up again in an hour. Jim Batten agreed to bring a broom handle and Ted said he had a roll of cello-tape in the office After lunch we discovered that Charlie wasn't feeling any more artistic than he was before lunch. Ted molt taped a four inch brush to the end of the broom handle, dipped it into the yellow and was passing it to Ibrahim when Charlie snatched it and promptly painted Elephant Jim's suede shoes! After a bit of coaxing and five minutes of speaking Indu, Ibrahim was finally sharing the broom handle with Charlie, but now couldn't reach the sheet of board. In his haste to get the board nearer to the elephant Jim Batten kicked over the can of red, with most of it going over Jim Warhurst's shoes. The transport yard was now an absolute mess and not being made any better by Elephant Jim tramping around in wet, paint-sodden shoes. At least 'Big Charlie' was now holding the broom handle.

After a quick consolation we all agreed that the board should be laid on the ground near Charlie's feet. Ibrahim got Charlie closer to the board and then using the broom handle, which they were both still holding, started running the brush over the board. I realised that this was not quite what Billy Butlin had in mind and we were going to finish up with a masterpiece created by an Indian mahout. After spending another hour making further unsuccessful attempts we finished up with two yellow spotted vans, paint spattered all over Teds office wall, the yard looking a disgrace and Elephant Jim was cursing about his ruined shoes. We also had a very irate Ted Molt, who suddenly yelled *"Bugger this I'm going home for me dinner!"* He grabbed the brush and angrily started daubing and splashing different colours all over the board. We agreed we couldn't admit to failure and put the board inside the garage to dry. Jim Batten stood back and surveyed the board, mentally deciding which three foot piece would be the best to cut off to send to Billy Butlin.

I have often looked back and smiled at the memory and the thought that somewhere in Los Angeles is a wealthy American with a colourful abstract picture on his wall. When asked about it he has proudly boasted that it cost a fortune and was painted by the largest Indian elephant in captivity. How deflated his pride would be if he only he knew his work of art had really been created by a peed off Butlin Transport Manager!!

Ibrahim and Big Charlie had spent many years together in India. They were totally devoted to each other and the relationship between them was tender and touching. Billy had been told that if Ibrahim died he would have to have Big Charlie shot, and if Charlie died Ibrahim would probably shoot himself. Ibrahim always slept in Charlie's shed and when it was time for Ibrahim to change Big Charlie's fetters it was touching to see how the elephant helped him: Ibrahim, sat on a stool and Big Charlie gently raised his feet so that he could transfer the chains from one ankle to the other. Jim Batten who had witnessed this said *"It was like a child holding up his feet for his mother to put his shoes on."* and while this took place Charlie gently rubbed Ibrahim's back with his trunk. Big Charlie and Ibraham were popular with parents and children alike - Ibrahim fell ill. Despite the best medical attention Ibrahim died and, from that day, Big Charlie began to fail and Billy Butlin was advised by experts that he should be put down.

London Zoo were contacted and asked the best way to do this and they advised that he should be gassed. The RSPCA were contacted and asked to do it as painlessly as possible, and they came to Filey. They made Charlie's shed air-tight and then led a hose from the exhaust pipe of a lorry into the shed - that was the sad end of Big Charlie.

Johnny, in his new role of camp comic, was first-class and Eddie was doing an excellent job in the sports stadium. Ronnie, Harry and Patsy were back in the swing of things, we had a good team of Redcoats and the camp was running like a well-oiled clock. Dave O'Mahoney had left Butlins and so Johnny wasn't keen to visit Skegness any longer. We had acquired a new compere, a lovely old pro' called Jack Reed. He was also a ventriloquist who, instead of using a doll as the dummy, used a number of large Toby Jugs. He had been in ENSA during the war entertaining the troops and his claim to fame was that he had once been engaged to one of the Beverley Sisters. He was a really lovable old rogue and I quickly became very fond of him and, being an old pro himself, so did Marten.

He quickly established a reputation for being over fond of John Barleycorn but he was sensible and never got tiddly before the shows. But Jack would have been the first to admit he most certainly did so afterwards. The man who looked after the Kodak Photo Kiosk was a keen boxing fan and we had got to know each other the previous season. He was a friendly bloke who supplied some of the Redcoats with cheap give-away photos. I introduced him to Jack and he asked for a supply.

One morning I was in the office quite early when Jack staggered in looking rather disheveled and it was obviously very much a 'morning after the night before.' *"I need your help Rocky, I need your help"* He was almost pleading. He came over to the desk and put down a sheet of four photos. The type you get by putting a coin in a photo kiosk. He explained that he had woken up in the ballroom in the early morning and taken the photos as a joke. *"I've been stupid"*. He continued *"Really bloody stupid and I only did it for a joke!"* I picked up the four photos and saw they were pictures of a man who had opened his trouser flies and photographed his willy. *"You know the man who services the kiosk Rocky. Can you have a word with him for me?"* I asked Jack *"Why would you want me to do that?"* Jack explained that when he took the photo's he hadn't thought about it but now realised the negative was retained by the machine. He was in a real panic and I asked *"But Jack how would anyone know it's you??"* He stared into space for a moment, then broke into a huge grin and, shaking his head in disbelief at his stupidity, walked out of the office.

I was loving the freedom of being on general duties and had become the house captain of Gloucester *"This is your handsome House Captain Rocky, wishing a sexy good morning to the mighty most illustrious house of Gloucester!!"*

With a great team of Redcoats we made a determined effort every week to win the house trophy and had a lot of fun doing it.

Every camp had a team of resident, professional entertainers. They were called the Resident Revue Company and entertained in the main theatre on three nights a week. The company also contained 12 revue dancers. An arrangement had been made that the girls could have board and accommodation on the camp in return for working 12 hours in red and whites.

The principle comedians in our revue were the brothers Gordon and Bunny Jay, nice blokes and very funny comics. At the start of the season Gordon had announced his engagement to a new Redcoat Margaret, who, in the stage name Leslie Cochran, had just come out of the show My Fair Lady.

Marten, one day, called me to his office to say the Colonel had phoned to tell him that on his last visit, Billy Butlin had been embarrassed by a couple who had a complaint about their accommodation and, instead of taking it to the right department, accosted Billy in one of the bars. Evidently both the husband and the wife had been drinking heavily and it had been a most unpleasant situation.

Colonel Brown had decided that in future I should join the entourage whenever they were on camp, not exactly in the role of minder but the Colonel felt that being known to the campers and wearing my Redcoat uniform, I could perhaps handle a situation better than a man in a suit. My first thought was that I would walk a respectful few yards behind the party but neither the Colonel or Billy were having any of that. When they stopped at a bar for a drink I stood to one side until the Colonel beckoned me and asked what I was going to have!

The season was once again drawing to a close and Ronnie had requested a return to Brighton. Johnny had asked to join him. I could see how it was in the Companies best interest to retain the pair of them. Ronnie was a gifted pianist who could be called on to do an act in any of the shows or, if needed, entertain an entire bar full of people for an evening. He was also a first class Redcoat. John was in a league of his own and absolutely outstanding. Like his brother Dave Allen, he was a handsome man, and a highly talented, natural born entertainer.

Tiff had confirmed that I was also being kept on again for the winter and I was absolutely thrilled and delighted. The end of season and closure of the camp always came around too soon and it was always a sad and emotional experience. I honestly don't know of any other industry where friendships could be forged so deeply and be so lasting. Once again it was hard saying goodbye to a bunch of dear close friends and the usual amount of tears were shed in doing this. I was to discover that choose how often you did it it never got any easier.

Chapter Ten

IN WHAT SEEMED NO TIME AT ALL I was behind the wheel of my car and heading for Margate for the winter. If I had been given a choice I would have returned to the Ocean but on the other hand Margate would be a completely new experience. Patsy had taken a job as hostess with American Airlines but we had already put the lid on our romance anyway. Part of her job had been entertaining visiting acts and celebrities and almost every big name in entertainment came to Filey at one time or another. After the shows it was Patsy's duty to take them for drinks and a meal. She was such a beautiful girl with a gorgeous figure that it was only natural that some of these "Show Biz Stars" would make a pass at her. Patsy was such a playful flirt and just wasn't able to resist their attentions. I am not saying anything derogatory about Patsy. Indeed there isn't anything I could say. Our relationship started to cool and we decided to call it a day. I think the situation became more tolerable when we both realised that our association wasn't going anywhere and we became, and parted just good friends.

The hotels shouldn't really have been called Butlins Margate, as they were actually in Cliftonville, a couple of miles out of Margate town. During the Second World War the coast line of Margate, Broadstairs and Ramsgate on the Isle of Thanet, was considered a high risk invasion area. The numerous hotels along the coast were empty throughout the war years and fell into various states of dilapidation. Some were in such a dreadful state of disrepair that it would have cost the owners millions to renovate them back to their pre-war standard but Butlins didn't have a history of silk and velvet wallpaper when a coat of emulsion paint would suffice! Billy knew he could restore them quite adequately, for his type of guests, at a much less cost. Four of these hotels were acquired in 1955 from a Company called The Nicholson Hotel Group these being The Queens, The Norfolk, The Florence, and The St George. Eventually Butlins would also acquire The Grand Hotel, The Queen's Carlton and The Princes Hotel, which would be used for staff accommodation. The St George Hotel had a lovely Olde Worlde atmosphere with black wooden beams and dark stained wall panels and it was decided that as well as accommodating Butlin guests it would also be open to the general public. Guests were allocated accommodation in a particular hotel but were free to enjoy the facilities of any of the others. At the end of the summer season with the reduction in guests, hotels would start to close. The Queens Hotel had a small theatre, a swimming pool and skating rink. The Grand Hotel had a very majestic ballroom and there was a pianist, Mabel Marks, in the excellent cocktail bar. The Norfolk Hotel housed the cinema and children's theatre. The Florence Hotel provided most of the games facilities and, in a nutshell, there was something for everyone. We had an excellent team of staff 'Big' Gus Britton the lifeguard, an ex- submariner who would in years to come be awarded an MBE. Leslie Glass, a 'wannabe' magician, who would later take the stage name Melville. Terry Herbert an established magician, who would eventually become the entertainment manager. Johnny Hubble, an excellent Pianist. Norah Clarke, the ultra-efficient secretary.

Louie Grant, compere and Skegness Camp Comic. Duncan and Mamie Menzies, brother and sister Redcoats from Ayr. The Band Leader was Bert Hayes, who was also MD of the popular children's TV programme Crackerjack, presented by Eamon Andrews.

After a most enjoyable Christmas at Margate, I was settling down to what I expected to be a few pleasant months taking me up to another opening at Filey.

I had an unexpected phone call from Marten to tell me I would be returning to Filey much sooner than I had expected. The recent craze of Marathon Walking had been inspired by a cranky woman, Dr Barbara Moore, who, to prove her nutritional beliefs walked from John O'Groats to Lands' End in the unbelievable time of just three weeks Amidst a blaze of publicity she had walked her way into the hearts of millions of people. Dr Moore, a London vegetarian, did the walk eating nothing more than vegetables, honey, nuts and fruit. Billy Butlin, well aware of the enormous publicity that could be obtained decided to organize the " Walk to end all walks" it too would be from John O'Groats to Lands' End,. which is generally considered to be the longest distance between the north and the south, officially 603 miles (970,434 km) That is has the crow flies, but it's been clocked by road as 930 miles.

Marathon walking is something that ordinary people felt they could do. The upper classes had their fox hunting, yachting and skiing. Others with some measure of skill could climb mountains. But any normal, reasonably fit person could walk and Billy decided to give them a chance. He threw open a challenge to anyone over the age of 18, and offered a £1,000 prize for the winner and £500 for the runner-up. Well over 1,000 entries were received, but I asked the question then and I must ask it again now, why have a marathon walk starting in Scotland in February? The weather turned particularly nasty just days before the event, with snow blizzards and enormous drifts. I had been called back to Filey, where, along with Tony Watson, Shops and Bars Manager, Bill Sandys, Catering Manager and Jack Waller Catering Deputy Manager together with Jim Warhurst Chief Security I was told I was to become a member of the Official Route Wardens team.

We were told that check points would be set up along the route manned by Butlin staff. The walkers would be given official 'cards' which would be stamped and signed at each check point. It was our team's responsibility to ensure this was done correctly. We would be transported between these points. The race started with over 700 people- although 200 withdrew on the first day. Some were in top hats or bowlers and sporting brollies, women in bonnets and hats of every shape, size and colour. There were dozens of newspaper reporters, photographers and TV crew at the starting point and it begs another question. Why start at five o'clock in the evening? Billy Butlin hated any form of public speaking and always said *"I have only two speeches - on short and one long. The short one is 'thank you' and the long one is 'thank you very much"*.

He was asked if he had any items of interest he could tell them, at this point he pushed me forward, as he hated talking to the press, saying This chap will tell you!" I hadn't expected it of course and so just made things up, telling them stories I thought would interest or amuse their readers. I told them that amongst the runners was a one legged man, a woman who was going to do the race walking backwards and numerous would be walking in Wellington boots.

That evening, after checking quite a few check points, we realised that we had a man missing. We split into pairs and went out in an almost raging blizzard to try to find him. We knew he hadn't reached the last check point so we walked in the direction of the previous one checking under bushes and shrubs at the sides of the road After an hour of this and finding nothing we returned, wet through and freezing, to the last check point. We were just in time to see Tony Watson and Jim Warhurst returning with a man who was cursing and struggling violently. I rushed in to help and grabbed the man's feet as he was kicking out wildly. Tony and Jim had found him in a shed under some straw. When we gave the poor wretch a chance to speak we discovered he was a vagrant who had curled up to sleep! After hot soup and a sandwich he insisted on returning to his bed!!

We eventually found the man we had lost fast asleep in the back of a van. He was caught the next day, between check points, riding in the van, just another of many who tried to cheat. During the first few day the atrocious weather sorted the men from the boys. We suffered gales, snow blizzards and the roads were lined with deep drifts. Men and women were dropping out at regular intervals. There were now ambulances all the way along the route for which Billy had felt disposed to make a "Generous donation". I found it amusing, at one of the first check points about 20 miles from the start, to be asked by competitors *"How far is it now?"* They looked at me in shock and astonishment when I replied *"About 900 miles!"* Lots of them had just no idea of the distance they'd signed up for.

The biggest problem we experienced was the large number attempting to cheat. Billy put about fifty cars on the route, all spaced about five miles apart, checking the numbers and times of all contestants. If we found anything unbelievable we disqualified the offender. At one point a section of the road was flooded ankle deep. A check point was set up a half mile further down the route. It was obvious that anyone who got there with dried footwear had been given a lift. At first we were catching cheats all along the way but that was the only way those type of people could have possibly won and the further we went the more we sorted the wheat from the chaff. Soon all the cheats and impostors had dropped out and all that remained were dauntless men and women with a grim determination to complete the course and win. One of the walkers was Yorkshire cross-country champion John Grundy and pretty soon it looked like being between Grundy and another Yorkshireman Jim Musgrave. At the end of the day it was James Musgrave who was the first to reach the finishing point at Lands' End with John Grundy coming a close second just over an hour later. But it was the first woman to cross the line who won the hearts of many. Liverpool hairdresser Wendy Lewis, who had shown courageous determination, crossed the line with 25,000 people cheering her home.

At the end of the day the cost to Billy Butlin was something in the region of £30,000 not including the £5,100 in prize money. But what value in publicity? The newspapers had been interested in the walk from day one and it had been written and spoken about every single day and throughout the day, for weeks it had never been out of the news. It had constantly been on television and the radio. Months later I would spend an evening in the company of Harold Vinter the Butlin senior press officer and ask him what the thought the publicity had been worth.

He told me it was something that just couldn't be estimated as it couldn't be bought. But if it could, Harold told me, many millions of pounds!! The Walk had been a tough but enjoyable experience, which I wouldn't have missed for the world but I was pleased to climb into my warm bed at Margate on the first night of my return. Margate was never really quiet, even the usually quiet two weeks before Christmas were fairly busy. Because by this time most of the other hotels had been closed due to a drop in bookings and the entertainment, dancing and cabarets had been confined to the St George, where they could also be enjoyed by the general public.

There was a regular guest at Margate, and I was told that he visited three and four times a year, he was affectionately known, amongst the Redcoats and other staff, as 'Champagne Charlie'. This wasn't for the amount of the stuff he drank himself but for buying champagne for others. He only ever came for a week and would buy a couple of bottles for the Redcoats every single night. He was a nice, quiet, retiring little man, rather shy and somewhat reserved. The staff decided that he must somehow have come into big money and eventually they all jointly agreed that he had won the football pools. I wasn't totally convinced as the quality of his wristwatch, shoes and other clothing, didn't suggest this. He came twice during my time there and on his second visit I felt that, although I had got to know him, I didn't really know anything about him. I joined him at his usual table, just before the start of the evening's entertainment, and presumed he was waiting for the Redcoats to appear to be bought their nightly treat.

By the end of our chat together I would know everything I needed to know and the entire situation would have been fully explained. In response to me enquiring if he was retired, he told me that he certainly wasn't and had a job that kept him occupied 24 hours a day. He explained, with some measure of pride, that he worked at London zoo and was in charge of the reptile house. Although he was anxious to stress that it was as much a hobby as a job as he had enjoyed a love and interest in snakes since he was a young boy. He told me that the care of his snakes was a 24 hour job, over seven days a week. He explained that he lived on the job and one of the perks was a small rent free cottage. He told me that he didn't mind working seven days a week as he had such a love for his snakes. They made it up to him by paying him overtime every week and by giving him four weeks off with pay every year. When this happened they had to bring in a reptile expert from another zoo to tend the snakes. So much for this kind, generous little man having won the pools!

The Butlins Royal Albert Hall Reunions were one of the main events of the winter. Most of the day, as I recall, was taken up filming highlights of the Butlin Beaver events for children's television, and were usually presented by Marten Tiffen. Lots of the evening was taken up dancing to the Eric Winstone orchestra for Modern and Harry Davidson and his orchestra for Olde Tyme. I seem to remember they alternated throughout the evening. The Butlin National Veleta finals were also a featured as was, in the early days, the Grand Finals of the Butlin National Holiday Princess Competition. The Butlins Square Dance Team performed. Also Dee Piggott's Limbo Dancing Team of which I was a member. The Butlin Choral Society also entertained.

The highlight of the entire week was when the Duke of Edinburgh came to be presented by Billy Butlin with the cheque for the National Playing Field Association, of which Prince Philip was patron. There was always a large number of TV and Film Stars present for this and they marched onto the ballroom floor through a Redcoat Guard of Honour. One year I was detailed, with three girl Redcoats, to usher them, when they arrived individually at the foyer, to a VIP bar. That occasion must have been 1964 as I remember Stanley Baker was there and his latest film Zulu was running in the West End. Also at that one was Syd James, Barbara Windsor, Kenneth Williams, Charles Hawtrey, Joan Sims, Hattie Jacques, from the Carry On films. Also Jack Hawkins, Michael Caine, Jack Douglas, Terry Scott, Helen Shapiro Roger Moore, Bernard Breslaw, and Wilfred Bramble of Steptoe fame.

They were certainly nights to remember and there were other events too. Much more was made of the Butlin Redcoats in those days and they were rarely out of the news. Teams would go to special children's films shows at Odeon cinemas on Saturday mornings right throughout the country. The children would see a free film show and the Redcoats would organise a sing-song before the film. Reunions would be arranged in various towns at Top Rank ballrooms, and again the Redcoats would entertain with a similar programme to the Albert Hall. It was all about keeping continuity with the Butlin guests throughout the winter and it was done on a big scale.

A national newspaper did a census in the late fifties asking young people what particular job they would most like to do. It could have been Sportsman, Sportswoman, Air Steward, Stewardess, or Butlin Redcoat. Almost everyone said Redcoat and Butlins used to boast 250,000 applicants for the position every year.

It can't be denied that working the hotels in the winter and getting the opportunity to watch each other work gave the permanent Redcoats a distinct advantage over the seasonal Reds. You were able to study different styles, or personalities and see the way things were done on other camps. I have often heard Redcoats say that they learned whatever skills they had from their peers and counterparts. I would agree with that without question. I learned a great deal at Filey by watching Johnny and Ronnie. I had learned lots more at Brighton from Keith and Wally. I would have to admit learning throughout this winter from Terry, Leslie, and Louie Grant. I wouldn't go so far as to say that I blatantly pinched material from them but when we parted company I was always able to increase my acts by a good few minutes!!

Saying goodbye to your winter colleagues at the hotels was no easier than doing it on the camps. You had spent in the region of seven months together working in very close contact and forming friendly and lasting relationships. It was always sad to say farewell.

Knobbly Knees, Filey 1958

Children's Fancy Dress, Minehead 1962

Chapter Eleven

ONCE MORE I WAS BEHIND THE WHEEL OF MY CAR and heading north to dear old Filey. I couldn't have been more elated or in a happier frame of mind, Marten had sent my new contract and I was going back as chief Redcoat.

Ronnie Hunter was back again so was Harry and Johnny and lots of the old Redcoat team. I was pleased to be told, that by his own choice, Johnny was to become the camp comic. I was pleased I hadn't taken his job. I asked for a meeting with Marten to discuss a few points I had been thinking about. In those days a chief Redcoat's responsibilities were much greater than they would become in later years. The entertainment department's staff was much larger at that time and the management team consisted of the entertainment manager, his deputy, two assistants and a trainee assistant manager, allowing this large number of people to give instructions to the Redcoats would be like asking a committee to design a camel. It had been decided some years ago that every facet of the Redcoat team would be the sole responsibility of the chief Redcoat and if the management team saw any misdemeanors, or had anything they wanted to bring to their attention they would tell the chief Redcoat. To do the job, as it should be done, was very demanding and totally time consuming. I had always thought it was a good thing to have a chief sports organiser or CSO. He would have the responsibility of organizing all the sporting events and that included the swimming gala and sports day. I didn't feel it should be the responsibility of the chief Red to check out the netball, tennis and soccer or be tied up, for hours on end, at a sports meeting or gala. Apart from that a CSO would be another pair of eyes. I had discussed this with Ronnie some time ago and he had agreed with me. I was aware of his love of sport and how he enjoyed being MC on sports day and the swimming gala. I broached him on the subject and he said he would love the job. We both knew that his prime position was Redcoat entertainer but becoming CSO wouldn't affect that in any way.

I also wanted to talk with Tiff about the pre-opening meetings. I agreed that the full induction meeting for new Redcoats was an excellent and necessary thing. It was most helpful to new Reds and gave the person taking the meeting the opportunity to stress the importance of good time keeping and other aspects important to the department. If the time of the meeting with new Redcoats could be lengthened it would give an opportunity to go into even greater detail about some of the more important points. Discussing all those points with experienced Redcoats was like teaching your granny how to suck eggs! They had heard it all before and were well aware of things. I was delighted when Marten agreed on both counts. I dashed off to give Ronnie the good news. We had eleven new Redcoats and I arranged a long session explaining important aspects of the job, what could and what couldn't be done and what should or shouldn't be done. They were attentive, interested and wanted to learn and it was far, far better than seeing a couple of dozen others looking as if they were 'watching paint dry'. I left the meeting feeling that we had a bunch of new people who would develop, with a bit of help, into an excellent team.

  This was the first season of the glorious 1960s. The years that were the absolute heyday of the Butlin theatre, when every camp had a family theatre presenting good, clean fun and entertainment. Billy was still building theatres but bigger and even better. The theatres he was building now would seat 2,000 and some even had revolving stages. The jewel in the crown of course was still the wonderful Gaiety theatre at Skegness. The names of the artistes would change as the years went by, with every era producing its own show business stars. The fifties and sixties would see the marvellous talents of Rex Roper and Maisy, Kazbek & Zara, with Francoise and Zandra. Topping these excellent bills, in those early days, would be Jimmy Wheeler, Tommy Trinder, Monsieur Eddie Gray, or Reg Dixon. In later years we would see Arthur Tolcher, Doreen Lavender, The Bewildering Zodias and topping would be Eddie Calvert, Dennis Spicer, Arthur Worlsey or Charlie Cairoli. Later still Joan Hind, The Konyots, and the bill toppers would be Wynn Calvin, Kenny Cantor, Neville King, The Patton Brothers or Don McLean. With not a hint of blue material from any of them and shows that mum and dad could take the kids to, even with granddad and nan. They could all return later to watch a family film which were mostly new releases. From the programmes I have of the 1950s I see there was "A Kid For Two Farthings": "Lady And The Tramp": "Darby O'Gill And The Little People": From the 1960s era there was "Lawrence Of Arabia": "West Side Story": "Dr Zhivago": I made a written request to Colonel Brown for a new release "Born Free": And a few weeks later we were watching it together at Skegness.

The era of the seventies brought "Railway Children": "Airport": and "Mash" The films we showed at Filey in the 80s era were "Superman" : "The Black Stallion": and "Herbie Goes Bananas" There was no admission charge and all the shows were free.

Butlins had the proud reputation of being the largest employers of musicians and entertainers in the world. But apart from the talented variety artists performing in the resident shows, there were also tremendously talented visiting performers. The first who immediately springs to mind is the fabulous Roger Stevenson's Marionettes. Roger- known as The Master Puppeteer, started his puppet company in 1963 and is regarded as the leading Marionette Company in Europe. Roger and his puppets have performed all over the world. His success story stretches from his first highly acclaimed Royal Variety performance at the London Palladium in 1978. They have since returned for Royal Variety Shows no less than five times. Roger did his first summer season at the Butlin Metropole Hotel, in Blackpool, in 1963 and that led to an association with Butlins that continues to this day. In 1965 Roger was introduced to comedian Ken Dodd, and created string puppets of 'The Diddy Men'. Ken was using this group of characters in his stage show, but Roger created the puppet characters for television and stage. The first versions were seen on 'live' TV specials from The Opera House, Blackpool and in 1968 they appeared in the first of four series for the BBC. Roger later did 150 puppet programmes for Yorkshire TV but despite his phenomenal success Roger remains loyal to Butlins, and thousands of children and parents alike have thrilled to his regular Butlin performances.

Another of the great visiting acts was the tremendously talented illusionist, mind reader and hypnotist Maurice Fogel, or to give him his proper billing "The Amazing Fogel". Certainly the most outstanding showman I have ever seen in my entire life and quite probably the greatest showman in the world . I have heard him described by people well established in 'the business' as greater even than Houdini. Maurice was born in the East End of London, the eldest of seven children of a working class Jewish family. When he was a very young man he worked as an assistant to 'The Great Rameses -The Royal Illusionist .'

He always said it was this work that gave him the basics of showmanship. In the late 1950s in the Viennese Ballroom at Filey camp, he had a stall in a passage-way at the rear of the stage. At this stall Maurice would take the birth-dates and names of campers and, later in the week for the sum of two shillings (10p) he would provide their personal horoscope. I was introduced to one of his amusing little stunts before I had even met him.

At the entrance to the stall there was a large goldfish bowl, filled with a few pebbles and sea shells but no fish. At the side of the bowl was a sign that read "Invisible Fish-Please Do Not Feed". I was amused at the number of people gathered around looking for the invisible fish. It made me chuckle and I liked Maurice before I even met him. Maurice has been described as the world's most audacious mentalist. He read minds, hypnotised his audiences, dared death and he became a legend in his own time. He would invite on stage six marksmen to fire six genuine loaded rifles.

One of the men was asked to choose a rifle at random, from the rack which contained the rifles, and fire at a china plate, which he did smashing the plate to smithereens. The rifle was put back on the rack with the other still-loaded five. The rack was rotated until no-one could possibly know which was the empty weapon. Each of the six volunteers took a rifle from the rack. Five of the men were asked to aim at plates above Fogel's head-but the sixth man was told to fire at Fogel's mouth, then on his command they all fired. The plates would shatter, Fogel would stumble and then spit a bullet into the palm of his hand. He baffled the world and even fellow magicians for many years and defied death on a nightly basis. A number of his stunts were so bare faced that it was amazing how he got away with them. He fooled thousands of people and received enormous publicity for one of them.

He challenged four of the world's leading chess champions to a tournament, promising £20,000 to any charity if he didn't beat at least two of them. He placed his four opponents in separate cubicles, each with a chess board in front of them. Entering the first he invited his opponent to make a move, he then went into the second cubicle and made exactly the same move, he carefully noted the countermove and then, returning to the first cubicle he made that same countermove. He did the same thing with his other two opponents and the game continued to its conclusion without the four champions realising they were playing each other! Just as Fogel predicted he did beat two of them!! Maurice almost made a career out of Butlins, spending over 20 years entertaining millions of Butlin campers.

A selection of repertory plays were performed on all the camps and they were originally presented by The Forbes Russell Repertory Company. Forbes Russell himself was a most flamboyant character with a somewhat 'delicate' disposition.

He always wore a velvet cape carried a silver knobbed cane and was usually surrounded by a number of young men of the same type as himself. They presented an unbelievable programme of 12 different plays over a two week period. What marvellous experience for young actors just starting in the business, learning that number of scripts and then performing twice nightly over a 20 week season. One of those looking for that sort of experience was John Inman. Aged only 13 John made his stage debut in The Pavilion, on Blackpool's South Pier, in a melodrama entitled 'Freda'. At 15 he took a job on the pier, making tea, cleaning and playing parts in plays. He came to Butlins Filey in 1957 aged 22. John was very effeminate when he was a youngster, and one evening on the way to the theatre he was accosted and insulted by a couple of lads on the staff. Whatever had taken place had reduced young John to tears causing the play to start late. The incident occurred before the first house and so disrupted both houses, as they both went up late. Joe Shaw was the stage manager and 'a bit of handful' and the incident ruffled Joe's feathers. Joe brought John to the marquee at lunch time the next day and asked me and Big Ken to go with them to the staff canteen to see if John could recognise the lads. He couldn't see them but our visit no doubt served its purpose. Joe was well known, as something of a tough nut, amongst the staff lads and the size of Big Ken spoke for itself. The staff now knew that John Inman wasn't on his own and had friends. His charming mother always insisted on taking me for coffee on her frequent visits.

The plays were carefully selected to appeal to our type of audience and the programme included "Bell, Book and Candle": "Sailor Beware": and "Night Was Our Friend". John, playing mainly juvenile leads, was excellent in Butlin repertory and, after gaining a couple of years' experience on the camps, went on to have very varied and distinguished career. He established himself in leading theatres throughout the UK as a first class pantomime dame. Then, as Mr Humphries with his catch-phrase "I'm Free", in the popular British sitcom "Are You Being Served", which ran from 1972 to 1985, he became a household name, winning numerous awards including BBC TV Personality Of The Year.

Once again it had been proven that Butlins was the greatest

nursery for budding talent in the entire world, even for those in the acting profession.

To complete the story of repertory at Butlins, and its very sad demise, I think it's now necessary to go forward in time a few years. Michael McDonna, was the general manager of the Forbes Russell Repertory Company, and David Kennington was senior producer. Michael later bought out Forbes Russell, and David became his partner. Michael and David were partners in real life and had been together for many years. They renamed the company 'The Albany Players', but sadly within a few short years, around the mid-1970s, audiences for the plays started to drop. The advent of TV was thought to be the cause and it was realised that in its heyday, when repertory at Butlins was thriving, nobody who came to Butlins on holiday had a TV. Suddenly every home in the country had one and the family could watch leading films, drama's and plays every night of the week. Every effort was made to save the plays, performances were cut to once nightly, but it was all to no avail. The Albany Players were pulled out.

For anyone not too familiar with theatre jargon the 'Get In' is when you are putting into the theatre the scenery, props, and costumes for a forthcoming run, be it a summer season or pantomime. Therefore the 'Get Out' is the complete opposite. I had a phone call from David to say he was coming to do the 'Get Out' on a particular day and it was a very sad occasion for everyone concerned. Joe Shaw, the stage manager, had been responsible for the three Filey theatres for a number of years, the stage manager of the Playhouse had been with the repertory for 3 or 4 seasons, and not the least sorry were David and I.

We had worked closely together for quite a number of years. David arrived in a large vehicle and with about six others helping we quickly loaded the flats, furniture, costumes and everything else that had to go. Again for the benefit of anyone not too familiar with the workings of repertory, every theatre has, backstage, a solid wooden box, it's about 2ft square and has a heavy lid on strong hinges, door knob is attached to the lid, the box stand on its back with the lid uppermost. Whenever a character in a play leaves a room through a door, the lid is lifted and closed heavily. This is a prop called 'The Door Slam' and its use will be obvious. It was the last thing to be brought out by one of the stage hands, he placed it on the floor at the rear of the lorry. I watched, almost with a tear in my eye as David opened the lid and 'Slammed' it for the very last time!!

In conversation with Marten, one day, he told me that he wanted to put on two late night shows in the Empire theatre. He wasn't happy with the audience attendance for two of the films and he wanted to replace them with live shows. The nights he wanted to present them were Tuesday and Thursday, the shows would start at 10.00pm and be of an hours duration. Johnny would present one of them and I would do the other. Johnny and I spent the next couple of days cajoling what we considered the best Redcoat acts to be in our respective shows. Johnny decided on the title 'O'Mahoney's Madness' and I settled for 'Rendezvous With Rocky'. At the end of the day we both came up with good shows but I always felt that Johnny's just had the edge. I had a snappy opening which Ronnie wrote, a catchy tune and just enough to get the show started.

Rocky, Rocky, on with the show,
Razzmatazz, and away you go,
Rocky, Rocky, make them laugh,
That's the reason you're on the staff,
So now the time has come let's go,
The Rocky Mason Show!

As chief Redcoat I was able to persuade some of the best acts to join me in the show. Martin De Mullen, an excellent act on piano accordion, who opened the show and finished his spot playing 'The Dam Busters March', with spotlights panning around the walls of the theatre like wartime searchlights. Frankie Barry did an excellent ballet routine. Robin & Terry Gee, on drums did their 'Battle Of The Bongo's'. We had a nice selection of sketches, but the *piece-de-resistence* was dear Ronnie, in black tie and tails, playing classical numbers on a grand piano!!

The campers had an image of Ronnie, sitting at an upright piano, stomping out his signature tune "Bill Bailey". They were shocked to see him appear in tie and tails And play some delightful classical music.

Wally Goodman turned up one day quite out of the blue as Tiff wasn't expecting him. He was with Russ Hamilton and someone I gathered to be an agent. By this time Russ was quite a big name, having received his Golden Discs and the resultant publicity. Wally asked me to put Russ on the show and he said he would like to do three numbers, which was roughly 9 minutes and that would be fine. It was a wonderful treat for the audience and he brought the house down.

A number of Butlin traditions started to be phased out in the 1970s, 'Who's Who' in the theatres, where personalities were introduced to the audience, even 'Goodnight Campers' had been replaced by 'We'll Meet Again' and was only sung on Fridays. The customers were now called Guests and the term Campers had been long phased out. The signs over the bathroom and toilet blocks saying 'Lads & Lasses' had long gone. Through no fault of their own Redcoats coming along later wouldn't have seen those things and perhaps have only heard about the Knobbly Knees Contest, I will try to explain what it was about.

The Knobbly Knees Competition had for years been the butt of music- hall jokes but, up to the 1970s it was always one of the most popular and entertaining competitions of the week. Johnny O'Mahoney often compered it, and I did it myself, and of course it was done, by someone or other, on all the Butlin camps. So, over the years, I have seen quite a number of interpretations of this particular contest. If I was asked to give an award for presentation, the winner would have to be the zany Mike Onions. Mike made a full scale production of it. Most of us got the contestants to roll up their trousers in front of the audience. Not Mike, in his contest they went behind a screen to roll up their trousers and when they came out from behind the screen they came out dancing! But more than that they were wearing colourful hair ribbons and tutus. Mike was into a laugh from the audience from the very start. He had a clever collection of stock phrases which he used throughout. *" You do realise that your wife has grounds for divorce?"* : *"I have seen more fat on chips"* : *"You have so many varicose veins it's like looking at a road map!"* : *"I'm not kidding I have seen more meat on a butchers biro".* But, his great *'Finale'* was when the winner was announced and would suddenly become the Prima Ballerina in the Bolshoi Ballet. The Prima would stand in the centre of a circle and her fellow contestants would dance around her, performing "The Dance Of The Dying Swans"…….. Mike would be encouraging….. *'Die with a bit of elegance.. Try to show a bit of grace".* It doesn't sound so funny now in the telling of it, but it was then or it wouldn't have become a tradition lasting for so many years.

Ronnie was happy and doing a great job as CSO, Johnny was his usual inimitable self, Eddie, Harry and Ken were doing a great job in the stadium, we had a superb team of Redcoats, all having a wonderful time. But suddenly the weeks were rolling by and we would soon be experiencing the sadness of yet another closedown and an emotional end to the season.

Johnnie was going back to Ireland to spend the winter near his family. Ronnie and I were to be wintered at The Ocean Hotel.

Chapter Twelve

I COULDN'T THINK OF A BETTER JOB, or a nicer way of life, for any young person, than spending the summer on a Butlin camp and going to one of the hotels for the winter. It was now 1961 and I had been with the Company five years and, by working at Filey, and four winters between Brighton and Margate I had met quite a number of important people and gleaned a fair bit of Butlin experience.

I considered myself to be a capable compere, performer and, hopefully, all round Butlin person. I knew without a doubt that this was where I wanted to be and what I wanted to be doing with my life and so when the Colonel asked me to go to see him at London Office, I felt nervous and more than a little apprehensive but mostly excited.

Colonel Brown was a big man, both in size and stature, but I knew him also to be a kindly man. Our meeting was to inform me that our newest camp at Minehead, Somerset, would be opening the following summer, it was going to be the new flagship of the fleet and I was to be the deputy entertainment manager. Colonel Brown took a small party of us for lunch. The party consisted of Wally Goodman, the Colonels assistant, Bill Martin who assisted Wally, and Maggie, the Chief Hostess. Also in the party was Daphne, the Colonel's secretary, an attractive lady who, in her younger days had been a Tiller girl dancing at the London Palladium. When the Colonel ordered champagne I thought for one silly moment it was to celebrate my promotion to the management team; it was no such thing and was to celebrate his engagement to Daphne. It also marked the start of what would, between us become, a long and wonderful friendship.

Minehead is a most beautiful, small Somerset market town and is the gateway to Exmoor National Park. It's a convenient stopping place for visiting some of the most delightful and interesting attractions in the West Country. Minehead is where Exmoor meets the sea and North Hill, where Exmoor National Park begins, dominates the area and its green slopes can be seen for miles. Just up the coast is Watchet with its quaint little harbour and excellent coastal views from the West Pier. Situated a few miles inland is the delightful town of Dunster, the jewel in the crown of Exmoor, with its delightful nunnery, dovecote, ancient packhorse bridge, the celebrated yarn market and, towering above all else, the majestic castle. Minehead camp really was a camper's dream-a luxury camp built close to the sea, just across from the harbour in the shadow of North Hill.

Al Harris was the Entertainment Manager and, to cover the massive amount of work needed to get the department ready for opening, Head Office had sent a number of senior people from the entertainment department on other camps. We were there essentially to prepare and equip various entertainment facilities but on arrival I could plainly see this was not going to happen. In example you can't put tennis nets out and mark the courts when they haven't even been built yet! Nor could you put table tennis nets up in a games room that hadn't yet been glazed. As I was going to be Deputy, Al Harris put me in charge of our work party and asked me to report to the General Manager.

Until such time as we were able to do work within our own department we would be seconded to camp management. One of the first jobs we were asked to do was in the indoor swimming pool, putting up plastic vines and trailing plants hanging from the ceiling. The iron girders holding up the roof had been boxed in with timber boxes simulating bamboo. The trailing plants would be contained in these. This method was used in a number of Butlin buildings to conceal exposed iron roof girders and the result was most effective. The vines were stapled to a 2" x 2" piece of wooden batten 4 feet long. There were four trailing plants to each batten. Only Bob Hastings, a Bognor Redcoat, Stan Howlett, a Redcoat from Skegness, Harry Greenslade, new to Butlins and a former Bristol barber, and myself were prepared to work on the high girders. Keith Ellam, and Jackie Cooke former Ayr Redcoats, with Matt Hattrick, new to Butlins and Ken Hopson, a Filey Redcoat, would staple the plastic plants to the battens. The job was pleasant enough and took us two weeks to complete. Bobby and Billy Butlin were constantly looking in on us and I was pleased that they both remembered my name.

Our next assignment was to hang hundreds of life size plastic seagulls from the same bamboo boxes. I had seen this in Filey pool and it was most effective. We chose to hang them on fishing line, strong but fine enough to not be seen. We decided the trick was to have the gulls on various lengths of line and to fix the line to different parts of the gulls back so that when hanging they would appear to be in flight, swooping and diving. Again it was a two week job and, when completed, Billy Butlin expressed his satisfaction and we were all delighted with our efforts. Our next job was much meatier and heavier work. We were given large rolls of underlay and rolls of green plastic that simulated grass, and instructed to lay an indoor bowling green. For all the jobs it had been necessary to pool our brains as none of us were in any way experienced in any of it. I contacted the suppliers of the bowling green materials and they sent us plans. The playing area had a low retaining wall and the carpenters had to install this before we could actually lay 'the green'. We were enjoying lighter nights and longer days and, as camp completion was way behind schedule, we were asked to work until dusk.

On the way home one evening, all of us worn out, we came across a lorry that had come off what would eventually be a road. At the moment the road surface hadn't been laid and it was simply churned up mud. The lorry had lost its load and I noticed it was much needed cement. The cement was in paper sacks, strong paper sacks, but still paper and it had started to drizzle with rain. I explained to the lads that we couldn't just walk on by. It was outside what would become the Regency Ballroom and at that stage no glazing had been done. We formed a chain and passed the bags through one of the unglazed windows. Suddenly Billy Butlin appeared and it was apparent that he had been watching us from a building across the road. He spoke to the lads in that strange Canadian-South African dialect I had become familiar with … *"I've been watching you men and you've done well. A good job, a good job!!"*

He then took me to one side and pulling a wad of notes from his back pocket he said. *"Good man Rocky, good man"* He put £15 in my hand at today's rate that was £272. And equals today £30 a man! There was lots of hard work but there were some lighter moments. There was just one small cinema in Minehead and the film, which had been showing all winter, was "Spartacus" starring Kirk Douglas.

It was a cheap place to go for a rest towards the end of the week when none of us had beer money left. It was always packed with people working at Butlins, and I am sure I had seen the film half a dozen times. You could look around the audience before the film started and it was all people you recognised, joiners, electricians, painters and building workers, all doing contractual work on the camp. I am sure we had all seen the film so many times we could have played the part of "Spartacus" with no problem. There was one gripping scene when the army of gladiators had been defeated by the Roman soldiers.

They were all crowded on the slope of a hill and the Roman Centurion shouted .. *"I only want Spartacus, if you give me Spartacus you will all go free. If not I shall crucify you all unto the gates of Rome!"* Spartacus raised his weary body and shouted ....*"I am Spartacus!"* The slave next to him stood and shouted....*"I'm Spartacus!"* Suddenly every slave on the slope was standing and shouting ....*"I'M SPARTACUS!!"* It was a very dramatic and moving scene.

There were no proper canteen facilities where we could have our lunch and the contractors had taken over one of the empty buildings. There was no glass in the windows and no door on the place, but it did have a roof to keep the rain off. There weren't any chairs as such and we all just squatted on empty drums, crates, or boxes to drink from our flasks and eat our sandwiches it was a pretty dismal way to spend a lunch break. One day in particular was very cheerless, bleak and pouring with rain, we went to the canteen and there was an air of utter dejection, with everybody looking gloomy and forlorn. I stood on a box and roared ... "*I'M SPARTACUS!!*" There was silence for a brief moment and then someone at the end of the room stood and shouted ... *"I'M SPARTACUS!!!"* .... then someone else and suddenly everyone in the room was on their feet yelling "I'M SPARTACUS!!" It caused a bit of hilarity for a few moments and for weeks after, when I was walking round the camp, someone, perhaps working on a roof would yell out to me......*"I'm Spartacus!!"*

As the buildings were completed and the camp started to take shape it was clear that Minehead was going to be an incredible camp. It seemed that Billy had taken the best features from the other camps and put them altogether here at Minehead.

North Hill could be described as one of the most up-market and desirable residential areas in that part of Somerset. Almost every house is detached with a large garden and imposing driveway. Being on a high level, before the camp was built, the residents had unrestricted, breath- taking sea views. When Billy Butlin applied for planning permission to build the camp there was a lot of fierce opposition and most of it from residents of North Hill. The protesters had a very astute organizer in the person of a former army Major, also a resident of North Hill. Without the interference of the Major, who was organizing the opposition with military precision, Billy wouldn't have had much of a problem as a Butlin camp had so much to offer a small town like Minehead. He had argued that the camp could only bring prosperity to local traders and shop keepers and had promised that a major building on the camp would become a Winter Social Club with swimming facilities. One other thing that would have been a tempting morsel to Minehead Town Council, would have been the rates the camp would have brought into the Council's coffers. I can't honestly give a true account of the rateable value of Butlins Minehead.

But I can give an accurate yard stick to enable readers to make their own comparison, like Filey camp Minehead has always been classed as 'one of the larger sites', and to give you something to go by, Filey paid £344,000 a year to Filey Council in rates! Please trust my figures and to assure you I haven't made a typing error, the sum was three hundred and forty four thousand pounds a year!!

I am quite certain that almost every single individual in the entire world has some sort of skeleton in their cupboard. Something they would rather not see discussed or made public knowledge. Some personal secret, light or dark, that they would prefer to remain hidden. The Major was really becoming a thorn in Billy's side and something had to be done. What the Major hadn't really considered was that he was dealing with Billy Butlin, self-made millionaire, with all the guile of a fairground showman. A private investigator was engaged to have a look into the Majors background and pastimes. Yes, Billy had been right and there were things in the Major's past that he would have preferred not to come out. Without going into sordid details, those who saw the report decided that certain things that were detailed were a good enough reason for the Major to have left Essex, as he had, and move to sleepy Minehead. I think the Major was given the ultimatum 'Don't pee on my parade and I won't pee on yours'. He suddenly withdrew from the protestors and nothing was heard from him again..

Jack Sudds, who was to be the Minehead Photographic Manager, and I had worked together at Margate and were friends. His section was still being built, but all his equipment had unexpectedly arrived at main stores. Jack came looking for me in a state of great anxiety explaining that he had no staff to move it. I went with him and saw heaps of chromium plated, expensive looking photographic apparatus and some of it still packed in cardboard boxes. There wasn't an empty building on the entire camp where this costly equipment could be stored. The security department's office, which would eventually be at the main gate, was another building still to be completed and security were temporarily housed in a large hut. One of the lads pointed out there was a space at the side of the hut and the hut was manned 24 hours a day. We moved it without a problem and returned to stores to ask the manager if he had anything with which we could cover the stuff. He loaned us a pile of used blankets, which he explained were from the staff lines at Clacton, he also gave us a large tarpaulin sheet. A week or so later we moved Jack's equipment into his new building but one of the lads just dumped the staff blankets outside main stores. After a couple of days of rain I was walking past the pile when Billy Butlin called me over to him saying *"Somebody's dumped these perfectly good blankets and all they need is cleaning. We'll fold them and get them inside"* I certainly didn't tell him the culprit was one of my team. We started to fold the rain sodden blankets together and halfway into the job I realised that my hands were filthy, and a greasy, black scum had formed under my nails. We had just finished folding them and I was preparing to take them into stores when a Butlin van stopped and I saw the driver pass to Billy a newspaper parcel. He unwrapped the parcel and I could see it contained fish and chips, he promptly sat down on some sort of crate.

I thought of the state of my own hands and I knew the Guvnor's must be pretty much the same, as I carried the wet blankets into stores I glanced across at Mr Butlin and realised I was watching the undisputed King of the holiday camps, the world's greatest showman and self-made millionaire eating fish and chips out of a newspaper and contentedly licking his fingers!!

There were some marvellous characters amongst the locals and no one more amusing than Dick, the local rat catcher and erstwhile poacher. He had a wonderful dry sense of humour and told some hilarious stories. The General Manager of the camp was Joe Chisnell and he bought a large house on the outskirts of town. One day whilst walking in the vicinity, I bumped into Dick and pointing at the house he said *"That's Joe Chisnell's house -your General Manager, and that man owes me money".*

When I asked Dick to explain he said, *"He told me he had some moles come up in the middle of his lawn and he asked me to get rid of them for him. So I did-I killed the moles and repaired his lawn, then I saw him a few times and he never offered to pay me".* I felt sorry for Dick and said, sympathetically, *"So, what did you do then Dick?"* Dick said *"I called at the house and saw Mrs Chisnell and she said 'Oh no you must have made a mistake Dick we've never had any moles!"* I asked *"So what did you do then?"* Dick said

"I told her yes you did have moles and not only did I kill them but I repaired your lawn! But she says 'No you are wrong Dick- you have to speak to Mr Chisnell".
I asked Dick if he'd spoken to Joe Chisnell and Dick said *"I spoke to him and he said he had never had any moles. He said 'I've never had any moles and I'm paying you nothing!"* I asked *"So what can you do Dick?"* He replied *"There's not a lot I can do about it, but I'll tell you what boy... he's got some now.. He's got moles now!!"*

The day before the opening date when the guests would be arriving I walked around the department for one final last minute check. I looked in on the games rooms for billiards, snooker and table tennis. I checked the darts area to see that dusters and chalk were available, the tennis courts and sports fields. The TV lounges, skating rink, theatres and table tennis and I was delighted that every venue was spick and span and ready for opening. Sadly it couldn't be said for all departments. It had been decided that the first family to book in at reception would be given a free holiday for the following year. I had been nominated to meet them with a bunch of flowers. The press officer and a photographer would also be there as there should be some publicity in it for us, certainly in the families hometown newspapers.

We had an excellent team of Redcoats and it was great to see all of them in brand new uniforms! We had around ten of them in reception to greet the first arrivals and there was such a tremendous feeling of excitement the place was buzzing with it. Sadly, but I suppose it was to be expected, we experienced quite a number of problems. Not from our department as our side of things ran smoothly and without mishap. Some of the problems could almost have been called amusing. There were a couple of incidents of campers returning to reception with their chalet key and complaining *"This isn't really much use to us as there's no door on the chalet!"* The thing that saved the day was the fact that the camp was only at half capacity and we had empty chalets to re-allocate people.

That night it was wonderful to see the buildings suddenly spring into life. I checked both houses of the Gaiety theatre, and it was a joy to see the Welsh comedienne Glady's Morgan And Family, playing to almost full houses. "I gave the lodger a boiled egg for his tea. Me and the kids had egg soup." The Pig and Whistle bar was almost packed to the doors, with a trio playing on stage. The six rotating carousel cocktail bars were full of people sitting on bar stools, getting a panoramic view of the entire bar as the carousel slowly rotated. I crossed the bridge over the stream in the beautiful Beachcomber, admiring the thatch and bamboo effect over the bar, the gorgeous palm trees and other Beachcomber decor. I checked the storm effect machine and all was working well. I looked in on the Princes ballroom and saw dozens of happy people dancing to the Eric Galloway orchestra. The same applied to the old time dancing in The Regency.

I was delighted to find that I didn't suffer much of the wrench I had expected, being taken out of red and whites. Keith Ellam had been at Brighton when Brett had used my spot for the Redcoat Show Finale and spoke to Al Harris, who decided to use it in the show. It was much the same as it had been at Brighton but this time we had thirty Redcoats, on a rostrum behind me, singing in accompaniment. Al Harris was keen on Redcoat Bar Shows, and throughout the week we would do Old Time Music Hall, Maria Martin, and The Minstrel Show, I found myself in all of them.

After months of hard work and an investment of £2 million, Butlins Minehead was up and running. As the years rolled by a further investment of £11.2 million was made. The figure was so high due to 20 years of inflation. I had the pleasure of returning to Minehead to open The Museum, after I retired from the Company, some 25 years after the camp first opened and was pleased to see all the original buildings were intact and little had been altered.

Towards the end of the season we had a visit from a film crew together with the actors Ian Hendry and Janette Scott. Also with the company were twelve absolutely beautiful girls, who would be extras in the film. The film was about bathing beauty competitions and was called 'The Beauty Jungle'. I was the liaison between Butlins and the producers. During one scene these beautiful girls paraded around the outdoor and I saw they were all wearing sashes on which was printed the name of a town, who I supposed they were representing. "Miss Leeds", "Miss Blackpool" and so on, the one that caught my eye was "Miss Bristol", in my view the most beautiful of them all. I made it my way to find that her name was Marty. She had a stunning figure and a most beautiful face. I decided that I must somehow get to meet this gorgeous girl. But, no such luck, suddenly the filming was finished and the girls were whisked away by coach.

During the winter a covered walkway was built from the main gate to the Regency Building, which housed the indoor swimming pool, games room, bar and ballroom. This would become The Winter Social

Club, where, for a token membership fee, the locals could enjoy all the facilities of the club throughout the winter We presented filmed horse racing, cash bingo, cabaret and dancing and the locals had never seen anything like it. I was the Club Host, and compered the horse racing, cabaret and other events and I also did square dancing and party dances. There was hardly a Sunday that I wasn't invited to join a family for Sunday lunch!!

The memories I have of Minehead camp, the town and the locals are all very happy ones! With perhaps just one unfortunate blemish. Half way through the season I became aware of complaints about the noise and bright lights of the camp by residents of North Hill. Officially, of course, none of this was my concern of mine but to satisfy my curiosity I drove up one evening to take a look. I just couldn't believe my eyes and ears, the sight was appalling; I was looking down on a conglomeration of different coloured lighting. Red flashing neon outside the disco, other colours of neon on various buildings, a vast assortment of multi-coloured lanterns over camp roads and strings of multi coloured fairy lights round the edge, and on the islands, of the boating lake. The noise was atrocious. A cacophony of sound from the disco and ballrooms, mixed with a throbbing bass sound from the Rock 'n' Roll ballroom. I have to say, for anyone sitting in their gardens on North Hill it would have been unbearable. I am quite sure, over the years, the local shops, pubs and traders have done well from the camp but, in fairness I have to say, I sadly feel the residents of North Hill on North Hill paid a damned high price for it!

Looking back, with the advantage of hindsight, it seems that Butlins policy for their entertainment managers was to give them experience as deputies. Then move them onto the management of smaller centres, therefore grooming them in management before giving them the responsibility of managing the department on a camp. On reflection that was certainly so in my own case. The Colonel had written me to advise me that I would spend the winter as entertainment manager at Cliftonville, Margate.

Old Time Music Hall Filey late **1970s**

Filey 1959.

Goodnight Campers: Louie Grant, Red Brigden, Yvonne Glass, Johnny Hubble, Les Glass aka Melville, Norah Clarke, Rocky, Elizabeth, on mic' Jack Reed, on violin Charlie Palmer

House Captains Group Photo. Filey 1959

The cannon of death, perhaps the greatest redcoat gimmick of all time, which I always got the credit for - but I only built it. The idea was totally Johnny O'Mahoney's. This was at Minehead, but I also built cannons at Filey and Pwllheli.

Alan as 'Charlie The Waiter' and Rocky as 'Billy The Bouncer' Margate 1959.

My dear friend Harry Griver, ABA Lightweight champion, Army Imperial Services Champion, Golden Gloves champ. Fellow Boxing Instructor Filey 1957 and chalet mate.

Junior Fancy Dress, Minehead 1962.

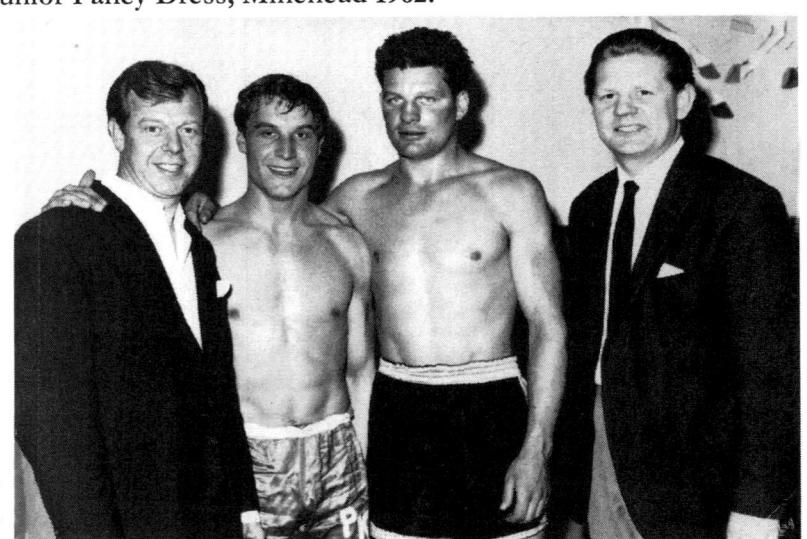

With Bill Martin after refereeing an exhibition between Peter Kane and the renowned Jack London, Pwllheli 1964.

Al Freid Musical director.One time MD at the London Palladium and MD of Moss Empires, brilliant musician.

Holiday Princess Southern Area Final, Margate 1963. Marty in striped costume.

Stan Stennett, Sunday Variety Comedian with Duke of Edinburgh Award boys, Pwllheli 1963.

Eddie Calvert 'The Man With The Golden Trumpet' and boys of the Duke Of Edinburgh Award Scheme. Pwllheli, 1964 ish.

Marty with Sheila Wilson, Bognor 1965.

Marty with her friend Anne Sydney after Anne became 'Miss World' with Eileen, Skegness around 1966

With Bill Martin, Alan Stratford Johns, TV's popular Inspector Barlow.

Marty, Chief Hostess, Skegness 1966 doing a bit of moonlighting!

Marty moonlighting again with Freddie 'Parrot Face' Davies. Skegness 1967.

With Edmund Hockridge, Sunday Variety Artiste and the Pro, Skegness 1967

Marie De Vere Dancers and members of the revue.

With Ray Fell and Billy Burden with two revue girls and Terry Moore. Skegness 1968

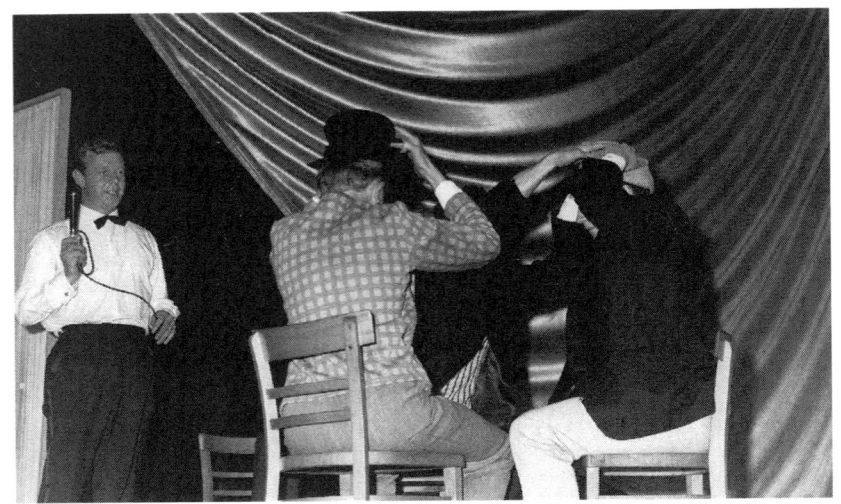

Musical Hats. Always a good laugh on the Lucky Dip show.

At the bar. The Ocean Hotel Brighton, Red Brigden, two brewery reps and Jimmy Noone who would eventually do 39 years there. I was Entertainment Manager.

Laurie Boynton.. Former Redcoat and Accommodation Manager Barry.

With regular visiting comic Freddy Sales, "It A Pooon" Skegness 1967.

Marti Chief Hostess, Skegness late 1960s.

Butlin favourite Ken Platt "I won't take me coat off I'm not stopping!

In his Redcoat days, dear friend Tony Peers, The talented young comic who went on to replace me as Butlin Senior Compere. He became a regular TV actor, Sunday Variety and Late Night Cabaret performer. Later, as an impresario, he became a Freeman of The City of London and Scarborough.

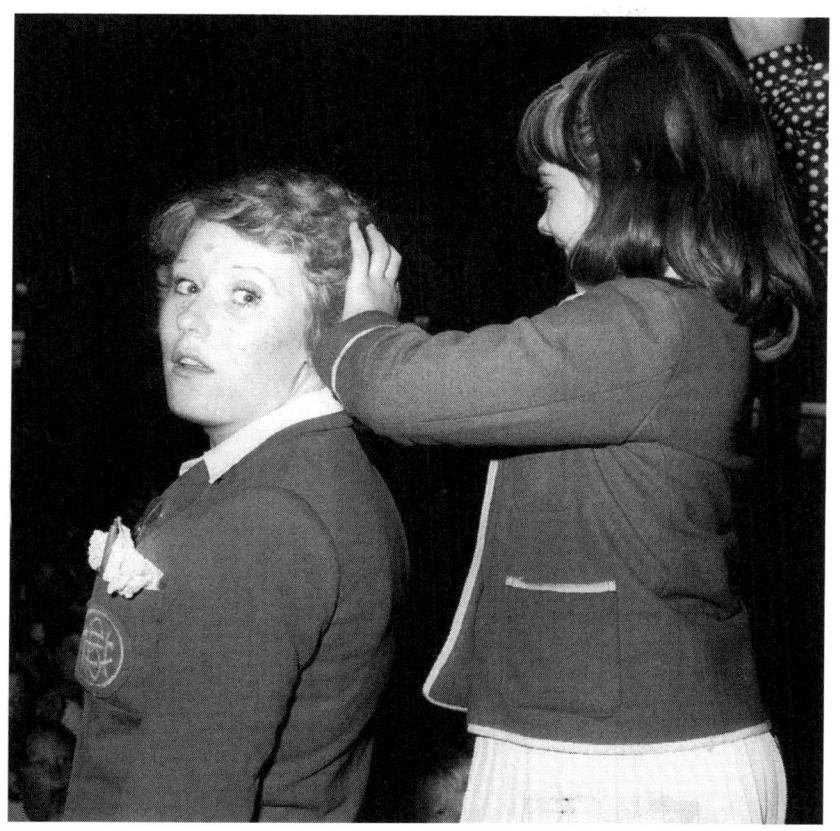

(Sam in red blazer when young). ... Sam, the youngest Redcoat at Butlins and had a contract to prove it!!

We did many happy seasons together. The dear, charming and funny Kenny Cantor.

Dear mate Neville King with the infamous Old Man Doll. In my view the funniest man on stage or off that I ever met in my life and I met them all.

Those were The Days - front row L to R Paul, Julie, Cathy, Chris Terry.
Back row L to R Rocky, Alan, Liam, Peter, Chas, (?) George.

As Frank Mansell would say "You're never completely dressed without a smile."

Midnight Cabaret

Here are a selection of some of the national star performers that graced the Butlin's stage during the "Big Night Out !"

The Batchelors regulars on Sunday Shows and Late Night Cabaret.

Mike Reid: The brilliant cockney comedian.

Regular visiting Sunday Show comedian and Late Night Cabaret.. George Roper.

Charlie Williams, Neville King, Ray Merrell, Frank Carson. Filey Late seventies.

Bob Marty and me, Late Night Cabaret, Filey 1979

Other Famous Stars who appeared at Butlins.

MAURICE FOGEL

The greatest showman I ever met

My good friend Richard Dunn, former British Heavyweight Champion, European Champion, Commonwealth Champion and who fought the legend Muhammad Ali for the world title

Julie Rogers, former Filey vocalist with Teddy Foster sold 15 million copies of 'The Wedding'.

Marty, Chief Hostess with Sunday Show regular Donald Peers

Dear Dave Butler, former Redcoat and later Revue comedian, appeared on TV in "The Comedians" and had a long run at the London Palladium.

Chapter Thirteen

ALL THE REDCOATS ENJOYED PERFORMING in the Queen's theatre at Margate, it was small and intimate, seating around 500 and situated in the basement of the Queens hotel. About 50 yards seawards of the hotel was a large bandstand where, often on a Sunday afternoon, visitors could sit in a deck chair and be entertained by a brass band. It could become quite warm in the basement and, on a sunny evening, we would often open the theatre windows. One Easter on a particularly warm, sunny evening Rob Wilton, a popular, Music Hall type of comic was topping the bill. The Bert Hayes orchestra were in the pit. Rob was perhaps five minutes into his act when suddenly a large, and rather noisy brass band struck up a rousing march. The duty Redcoats quickly dashed to close the windows. But the noise was still terribly distracting. What wasn't realised at first was that the music was the overture for a fireworks display. Then, without warning, rockets and bangers started exploding with thunderous bangs. Rob, looking totally bewildered, leaned forward over the orchestra pit and muttered the immortal words *"Bert, I think they're trying to train me to be a police horse!"*

It was the custom on Sunday mornings to invite the guests to join a Redcoat for a 'Coastal Ramble'. The objective was to take a party of guests on a pleasant stroll to the Captain Digby, a public house on top of the cliffs, and a popular local landmark. In principle the party would then about turn and return to the St George bar for the lunchtime sing-song. But in practice, subject to which Redcoat was in charge of the ramble, they would enter the Captain Digby to imbibe copious amounts of ale and spend money, that in theory, should have gone into the Butlin tills. There was just one non drinking Redcoat amongst the lads. Brian Mathews, a likeable cockney. It was on Brian's shoulders the 'Sunday Ramble' would usually fall. He was a born and bred cockney from East London, who had never even seen the sea until he came to Butlins. One day I was strolling along the shore at the same time as Brian and his party of ramblers. I saw him stoop to pick something out of the sand and his party excitedly gathered round clicking cameras. As I got nearer I was able to have a closer look at the object of excitement. It was a chickens head and neck and it was obvious that time and tide had washed away the feathers. I presumed it had been thrown overboard from a boat at sea. Unable to decide the reason for the excitement I said *" What have you got there Brian?"* His reply was in a voice steeped in authority *"A bleedin' sea horse that's what!"* He said with confidence *"It's a sea horse and you don't see many of these abhat - I have a pair of cuff links with this pattern on!!!"*

The Redcoats were always a joy to work with, hardworking, never late and very conscientious. Just before the start of Christmas, we had decorated all the venues and dressed the trees with baubles. The St George Hotel ballroom was the last one to be done and it took myself and four Redcoats the best part of a day to put the trimmings up. There were a number of round pillars down the sides of the dance floor and one of the lads had the idea of putting silver kitchen foil around the top of the pillar and cutting it in the shape of icicles. I didn't like the idea when he suggested it but the others wanted to try it. I liked the end result even less but didn't say anything as the Redcoat had meant well.

The next day the four same Redcoats came to my office to tell me they didn't like it either and would like to re-decorate the pillars. I explained that we had so many other jobs to do we couldn't afford the time they told me they realised that and were prepared to work into the night. It was so nice to see that they took such pride in their jobs.

Gus Britten, spent many years with Butlins after joining Pwllheli, in 1947 as a Redcoat Lifeguard. This followed his service in the navy as a Sub-Mariner. He was a very experienced seaman and held a Masters Certificate. Gus was in charge of the indoor swimming pool of The Queens Hotel. One day I had a phone call from the General Manager, informing me that a local school was expecting to use the pool and asking why I had closed it. I explained that I hadn't and there was no reason why the pool should be closed. I was informed by one of the Reds that Gus had decided to close the pool and accompany Brian Mathews who had gone to buy car. A substitute for Gus was found and the school were advised that they could bring their party. On his return I had no choice but to suspend Gus. I would later discover that a national appeal had been made for people with experience of sailing, they were wanted to crew a wooden built replica of a Viking ship to retrace voyages the Vikings had made around the world. Gus had been selected to Captain the crew. He had a hobby for drawing cartoons and was good at it. I became aware that the staff were showing interest in an item on the Redcoat notice board. I looked and saw it was a cartoon of the front view of a Viking, with his trousers round his ankles, sitting on a miniature Viking ship. Looking closer I saw a small 'PTO' printed on a corner. When I turned it over I saw a cartoon of the rear view of the Viking with his trousers round his ankles, showing his posterior and a message saying "Rocky Mason Can Kiss My Arse". Gus advised my secretary that he would be leaving at the end of the week. I didn't want to part not being friends as I had a lot of respect for Gus. I later saw him getting into a taxi and shouted across to him *"Good luck Gus!"* In reply he showed me two fingers! Some weeks later it was in the national press that the Viking ship had reached a beach in Spain. Gus and the crew had turned it upside down and burned it after Gus declared it un-seaworthy!

In 1995 Gus was awarded the MBE for his services to the Royal Navy Submarine Museum at Gosport, Hampshire.

Margate, with its many hotels, had a much bigger guest capacity than Brighton, but the principle was much the same, offering reunion weekends throughout the winter, and honeymoon weeks up until March. Redcoats were sent to Victoria station to escort guests coming by train. We then had coaches at Margate station to bring the guests to Cliftonville. Christmas and Easter were also capacity weeks. I should think the peak week capacity of Margate would be in the region of 1, 200, with Brighton around 800.

Anecdotes and amusing tales about the theatrical profession and people in it are called 'pro stories' and there is one in particular that has been doing the rounds for years. It involves a one-time-famous comedian called Jimmy Wheeler. He was one of the most regular performers in 'Variety Bandbox' the biggest radio show of the 1940s. In 1956 he had his own TV show "The Jimmy Wheeler Show" He always ended his act with his catchphrase 'Aye, Aye-that's your lot'.

Dear Jimmy had a reputation for 'imbibing' and on occasions far more than was good for him. I had heard a story about Jimmy and, when I asked him, he was more than happy to confirm that it was true. He had a daughter who lived in Paris and on one trip, for what was going to be a weekend, he got on the plane sozzled. He fell asleep snoring loudly and, on the pretext of offering him a drink, the stewardess woke him to ask if he would like a drink from the free trolley. Jim said *"Free drink? What do you mean free drink? You don't get a free bar on a Paris flight!"* The stewardess, now looking alarmed said *"Paris? Sir this plane is going to Karachi!"*

Dear Jimmy was booked to do Christmas Eve in the Queens Theatre at Margate. Sadly, travelling down by train, the worst thing that could have happened to Jimmy did happen. He was recognised on the train by some people also on their way to Butlins Margate, of course they were going on holiday and enjoying their trip, unlike Jimmy who was going to work. Somehow they got Jim to the theatre, but he was in no fit condition to do a band call. Having played for him on numerous occasions, Bert Hayes knew his act, and passed round Jimmy's music and I took him up to a bedroom. I threw him on a bed about 3 O'clock, hoping the three hours before the start of the show would be enough to pull him round. I woke him with one of the Redcoat girls, with hot black coffee, about 6.15, as Jimmy was down to top the bill he would have been going on stage at around 7.10. I had to leave them as I was compering the show, which started at 6.30. Jimmy looked as though he had slept it off and I thought he would be OK. When he came back stage an hour later I would have said he was fine to do the show. I spent a few moments chatting with him just to check him out and he seemed perfectly alright. I introduced him and he went to the centre mic to start his act, but suddenly just fell forward over the footlights. I dashed out and grabbed his legs as he was sliding into the orchestra pit. With Bert Hayes pushing and me pulling we managed to get him back on stage and up on his feet, it was then that he uttered his famous catch phrase *"Aye, Aye - that's your lot.* Then Jim made his sad exit side stage.

It had been decided to present the Southern Area Final of both the Glamorous Grandmother and the Miss She competitions at Margate, and I was pleased to have been asked to compere them both. They were always special occasions with celebrity judges and there was always a hospitality room and a superb dinner. I had spent some time with a couple of the lads preparing the sets and the competitions had gone well.

I felt, and I am sure the Butlin staff of any department would have agreed, it was a dream come true. Working on a camp, in the department of your choice, throughout the summer and then transferring to one of the hotels for the winter.

It's just a pity that so many other loyal Butlin staff couldn't share the privilege and there were certainly quite a number worthy of it.

On his last visit the Colonel had told me I would be returning to Minehead for a few days. We were presenting the televised Finals of the "Miss TWW Beauty Competition" TWW was the abbreviation of 'Television West and Wales' and the studios were in Bristol, the semi finals had already taken place and we were presenting the finalists who were representing their home towns in the South West, all in the viewing area of TWW.

Minehead was within this area and it had been decided to present the finals from the camp's Princes ballroom. At rehearsal on the Saturday morning of that evenings show I was attracted to one girl in particular and I seemed to know her from somewhere. It wasn't until I had the girls lined up in front of the TV cameras that it came to me! She had been one of the gorgeous extras in the film "The Beauty Jungle". There were 20 girls in the competition and the hostess had written their names, with other information about them on small, numbered cards. I returned the girls back stage to be presented individually and started to introduce the panel of judges, the famous British journalist, writer and actor Godfrey Winn, also Jimmy Greaves, the former Tottenham and England footballer, the well-known comedy impressionist Janet Brown, and the former host of 'Opportunity Knocks' and 'Double Your Money' Hughie Green, together with Barbara Windsor the star of 'The Belles of St Trinian's' and the popular 'Carry On' films. The competition went well, 'my girl' was number 17 and I discovered, from her card, she was 'Miss Bristol', 'Miss English Rose' and 'Miss Pink Lady of Great Britain' and her name was Marty. I was surprised and disappointed that she only came third.

At the end of the show I had to spend a few minutes with the show's producer and Colonel Brown, but I was anxious to get to the Green Room to join Miss Bristol. I was in there maybe six or seven minutes after Marty, to find Jimmy Greaves was already chatting to her. I had read something about Jimmy being a prolific scorer and a very fast player and whoever wrote that wasn't kidding! I got the Press Officer, who was a mate, to interrupt them with the story that he was a reporter with the Bristol Evening Post, wanted to do a piece on her but had a deadline to meet. Marty joined him and they went to a table away from the bar. I knew which barmaid to wink at to get a free bottle of champagne and joined them. Greavesy had been given a red card and was on the bench!….. 'It's a funny old game Jim.'

The room started to get smoky, noisy and warm and we decided to get some fresh air. Camp roads aren't really the place for a romantic stroll so we went to the beach and, for the first time in my life, I walked barefoot in the sand. It was around 11 o'clock when we went on the beach and we seemed to lose all track of time as we walked and talked. I was amazed when I took her back to her chalet and looked at my watch, it was four o'clock!

I felt happy and contented as I drove back to Margate, I had Marty's address and phone number safely in my wallet, she had promised to come to Margate and the Finals had gone well. Colonel Brown had told me that in a couple of months I would be moving to Pwllheli as Deputy to Bill Martin. We had met quite a lot at Brighton and become good friends. I had a suite in the Princes and a cheery little house keeper called Ada. Marty was soon visiting on a weekly basis and things were going well. Early one Saturday morning I had an urgent phone call from Wally, Colonel Brown's assistant, telling me to get to Bognor without delay as I was needed to compere the Finals of the Holiday Princess. The honour of presenting it had originally fallen to Kenny Lynch, a British film actor, comedian and close friend of Jimmy Tarbuck. For whatever reason, Kenny Lynch wasn't now doing the show. The journey took me about 3 hours and I arrived at noon. I had missed the rehearsals but was told the girls had been presented in exactly the same way as on the TWW Finals and so we shouldn't have a problem.

I was happy to be there for a number of reasons and not least because Marty was in the Finals. She wasn't placed but you can't win them all. On the drive back to Margate Marty told me that she'd like to come to Pwllheli. She saw a job offer in a newspaper and the job was for Butlins Pwllheli, she wrote to arrange an interview and got the job. She would be working for Philishave Electric Razors, and her title would be 'Miss Philishave'. She would be running 'the Philishave competition which would be held each morning at the Philishave Stand in the main shopping centre. The contestants would report to the stand in the morning and would shave in front of Miss Philishave who would then weigh their whiskers. At the end of the week the winner would be the one with the heaviest weight of whiskers. In the morning and afternoon, wearing her Philishave uniform she would judge a competition. This would take all of three hours a day and when I saw Marty's contract I just couldn't believe it - she was earning more than me! We excitedly started making or preparations for our move to North Wales, which would be a first for both of us!

Lucky Dip Show, Pwllheli 1963

Chapter Fourteen

I WAS ONCE AGAIN BEHIND THE WHEEL OF MY CAR and heading for another exciting Butlin adventure and this time to Pwllheli in North Wales. Within an hour or so we passed a road sign saying "Croeso Y Cymru"…"Welcome to Wales".

We tried to decipher place names like Blaenau Ffestiniog and others we couldn't even pronounce. We saw construction work in the Afon Tryweryn valley, to construct the enormous dam which flooded the small village of Capel Celyn. Almost the entire village was flooded. The village contained a chapel, with cemetery, a post office, the school, and twelve houses and farms were also submerged. Families who had relatives in the cemetery were given the option of either moving them to another cemetery or leaving them. Consequently, eight bodies were disinterred, and the remainder left. All headstones were removed and the cemetery was covered under a layer of gravel and then concrete.

Pwllheli was a beautiful camp bordered by mountains on one side and the sea on the other. It had its own railway station with the lines running right through the centre of the camp, it actually divided the camp into two parts. The two halves became known as North and South camp, and access from one to the other was over a bridge. The station was called Peny Chain, which the visitors called Penny Chain, almost as it's spelt, but the locals correctly pronounced it Pen -a- kine. At the end of the war after local opposition the camp wasn't opened until 1947. The miniature railway which was added in 1955 differed from those on other camps in that it fulfilled a genuine transport need. It ran for almost a mile along a most beautiful scenic route from the centre of the camp to the beach. The chairlift was built in 1960 and had to be the most picturesque ride of any Butlin camp. It ran from the camp down to the headland on the beach and the delightful views took in Mount Snowdon in the distance and Criccieth castle across the bay. Snowdon could clearly be seen from some parts of the camp and it was rather eerie on a warm sunny day in May, with all the Spring flowers in bloom, to look at the whiteness on Snowdon's peak and realise it was snow.

One disappointment I had with Pwllheli camp was that we had built a camp in the most beautiful part of North Wales, but it was totally lacking in Welsh character. I should have thought a Snowdon Bar and a Cymru Theatre would have been appropriate and appreciated by visitors to Wales.. Instead we had a Spanish Bar, Regency Ballroom, French Bar and Empire Theatre. I found it strange that there was nothing specifically Welsh and all of it in the very shadow of the jewel in the crown of North Wales, Mount Snowden.

During World War 11 the camp was subject to military occupation when it served as a naval base and became HMS Glendower. Prince Philip, Duke of Edinburgh, was billeted on the camp at this time.

In my view the only drawback to Pwllheli was the fact that it was actually two camps divided by the railway lines. If someone, on South Camp, was accommodated in the sports- field chalets and wanted to go to Midnight Cabaret in the Spanish Bar, on North Camp it was in the region of a half a mile walk. Likewise if a member of the entertainment management team checked bingo in the Coronation Bar on North Camp and then crossed the bridge to check the old time dancing, it was the same distance. Not pleasant on a rainy evening!

Billy Butlin had played no small part in the design and build of Pwllheli camp, just as he had on all the Butlin camps occupied by the military during the war.

The parade ground at Filey, had three 8ft entrances with a 4ft surrounding wall and, when the military left, the entrances were bricked up and the area filled with water, Billy had an ideal boating lake! By coincidence the parade ground at Pwllheli was just the right size for six tennis courts and surrounds!

Bill Martin was a good manager and easy to get along with. He was still, covertly, working as a comedian, in the name of Billy Vinden, I occasionally covered for him when he 'moonlighted' to do a Workers Playtime or Mid-Day Music Hall.

There was a situation on the camp in peak weeks that was unique to Pwllheli, when guest bookings on the camp were at absolute peak, for perhaps three or four weeks in August, the large number of campers couldn't be accommodated with just two shows in the Gaiety Theatre on North Camp. The acts had to do one performance in that theatre, then transport was laid on to take them over the bridge to do a show in the Empire theatre on South Camp.

Lots of visitors to Pwllheli used the camp as a base to spend their days touring that beautiful part of North Wales. Gwyned was home to some of the most delightful attractions in that part of the world. Beddgelert is a small village and a picturesque tourist attraction in the shadows of Mount Snowden. Swallow Falls is another popular visitor attraction, but so is, for that matter, the whole of beautiful Snowdonia. Caernarvon, with its historical castle, used for the investiture of the Prince of Wales, and the most famous of all the Welsh castles is just a short drive away.

The Revue Company was headed by Wynn Calvin 'The Clown Prince Of Welsh Comedy' and Wynn of course was an ideal act for Pwllheli camp, with Wynn was Joan Hinde, 'The Glamour Girl Trumpeter', Arthur Tolcher, with his harmonica, together with 'The Singing Walker Twins', 12 Revue Dancers were also on the bill. The Al Fried orchestra of fourteen musician played for the shows. We had a selection of excellent acts visiting for the Sunday Variety Shows and they included the ventriloquist Arthur Worsley, who appeared on America's Ed Sullivan show more times than any other artist and was reputed to have the most skillful lip control of any ventriloquist there has ever been.

'The Man With The Golden Trumpet', Eddie Calvert, who had big chart hits with 'Oh Mein Papa', ' Cherry Pink', and 'Stranger In Paradise' The wonderful singer Edmund Hockridge, who had starred with Geraldo, and the Glen Mirror Orchestras, also appearing in hit musicals such as Carousel, Guys and Dolls, and did a number of Royal Command Performances. Leonard Weir,the former West End star of My Fair Lady. Comedians Reg Dixon, Tommy Trinder, and Monsieur Eddie Gray, The talented up and coming ventriloquist Dennis Spicer, with his Corgi dog dolls, who was tragically killed on his journey home from a Sunday show at Pwllheli, when he crashed on the motorway with a man driving the wrong way!! Also the man I consider to be the funniest man I have ever seen on stage or off, the ventriloquist with 'The Old Man' dummy, Neville King.

The Head Gardener was Gwillum Edwards and, in my view, he kept the most beautiful gardens of any Butlin camp. His rockery and rose gardens were really something to see.

They were so acclaimed throughout all the camps that I used them for Staff Group photographs in three occasions. It's a well-documented fact that Ringo Starr played for the group Rory Storm And The Hurricanes, in the Rock Ballroom at Pwllheli just before he joined the Beatles.

HM Queen Elizabeth 11 made our first visit to Pwllheli something of a Royal occasion, when she paid a visit to her husband's old wartime posting. Billy Butlin personally escorted The Queen and Prince Philip through the various entertainment buildings, and introduced her to senior members of staff. Queen Elizabeth and The Duke of Edinburgh then got into the back of Military Police Land Rover, and were driven on a tour of the camp through crowds of waving campers. At the Queen's request they also visited the on-site church and met both the resident chaplain and Canon Tom Pugh, who originally brought the church to Butlins. I am sure Prince Philip would have had his own memories of the camp from the time he was billeted there. We had been told the Royal Pair would be taking the Royal Coach from Pwllheli station and the train would pass through Peny Chain. Colonel Brown asked us to arrange for the Val Merell orchestra to play on the station platform as the train passed through Peny Chain, but I thought the number Val played was hardly appropriate for North Wales, he chose "Will Ye No Come Back Again"

The Duke of Edinburgh's Award Scheme was an important feature at Pwllheli, and the camps geographical position made it ideal for this venture. The Duke of Edinburgh's Award Scheme is for youngsters between 14 and 24, but participants have to be 16 years old to compete in the gold level. The scheme is in three levels, which when successfully completed lead to a Bronze, Silver or Gold medal. It was Butlins responsibility to arrange for the participants and their leaders to go out on four day expeditions, and it was stipulated 'The expeditions should be for four days and three nights and should take place in 'wild country'. Usually between 8 and 10 youths took part with three or four leaders. Butlins provided camping equipment, rations and transport to the starting point of the expedition, which usually took place on Mount Snowden, which, of course was ideal for the situation. The party's visit to Pwllheli was the culmination of 12 months working on the scheme to qualify them.

Marty was really enjoying her job as Miss Philishave, and now working part time on Redcoat duties to occupy her evenings, and so the wages gap was getting even wider. After a couple of weeks I started taking a day off and Marty and I went out exploring the wonderful countryside. Running the entertainment on a Butlin camp is pretty much a full time job but we could occasionally arrange to meet at the chairlift station to enjoy the wonderful scenery on a ride to the beach. We managed to squeeze in a bit of social life together and occasionally Bill would suggest letting the two assistants 'put the camp to bed' and we would creep off to the grill room to have a meal together. Once the camp was into peak weeks, the staff and assistants were fully trained, we would often pop out for lunch in the next village, about a mile from camp it was stone built and quite beautiful, it was called Llanystumdwy. It was also the boyhood home of David Lloyd George, the former Prime Minister of the United Kingdom, who led the wartime Coalition Government between 1916 and 1922. So far the only British Prime Minister to have been Welsh and to have spoken English as a second language, with Welsh being first.

Llanystumdwy boasted a delightful pub called The Feathers, just off the river bank, and they did a marvellous crab sandwich.

We had befriended one of the Redcoat girls, Peggy Warner, and Peg' must have been the epitome of what Billy Butlin had in mind when he thought of Redcoat girls. Always beautifully and spotlessly turned out and her uniform and shoes always immaculate. Her trade mark was the brilliant white delicate lace hanky in her breast pocket, starched and pressed into a perfect shape and an Idea that was quickly copied by other Redcoat girls, Marty included. Peggy had a loud and infectious, laugh and was adored by the campers.

It was not widely known that Billy Butlin had a mansion just a mile or so from the camp, the house was set in the most attractive gardens and parkland and was called Broomhall. It had a private airstrip and Billy purchased additional land to lengthen the runways. Pleasure flights were arranged for visitors, using De Havilland Rapide and Auster Autocrat aeroplanes. It would have been a first experience for many who would never have flown before. The estate was purchased by Billy in 1946 when he was in the process of converting HMS Glendower into Pwllheli holiday camp. The resident Host was Major Frank Bond, and we had worked together during the preparation for opening Minehead. We became friends and occasionally 'The Major' would invite Marty and me to visit for afternoon tea.

Unlike his father Robert Butlin, or Bobby to his friends, seemed to have a desire to elude publicity and he certainly gave it a wide berth. When I decided to write my previous book "Gumshield to Greasepaint", we had both retired from the company and it took a lot of persuasion, on my part, to get Bobby to let me have details of his biography and early life. Bobby took over as chairman and managing director of Butlins Holiday Camps in 1968. He took over from his father Sir Billy Butlin, when traditional British summer holidays were undergoing a radical change. Cheap package holidays to Spain and Greece had been launched and holidaymakers had discovered the delights of getting on a plane to fly abroad. Going on a cheap package deal abroad was considerably cheaper than staying in this country for a Butlin holiday. Bobby was a shrewd businessman and one of his first tasks as chairman was to increase the publicity budget to start and an advertising campaign to lure back old, and bring in new, holidaymakers to the nine Butlin camps. He also introduced self-catering and put an end to the unpopular teenage block bookings, fading out Radio Butlins and, with the advent of self-catering, the now unnecessary Wakey-Wakey.

Bobby was born in 1934 and as a child he spent all his holidays on the Butlin camps. In 1951 he became a Redcoat at Ayr, later working as an assistant in the stores at Filey and Skegness. Bobby worked his way up in the business in an assortment of jobs. He was very much a chip off the old block. Bobby remained as chairman and managing director until 1984, even after the Rank take-over in 1972, when the company was sold for £43 million. It isn't widely known that Bobby was a Companion of the Grand Order of Water Rats, and a Director of Hendon Football Club.

Marty and I were delighted to be asked to go to the Ocean Hotel for the winter. She and Peggy had become good friends and I asked Peg' to join us, she was over the moon and lost no time in accepting.

Chapter Fifteen

I WAS BACK BEHIND THE WHEEL OF MY CAR AGAIN, after saying goodbye to beautiful North Wales, I was now heading for Brighton, to run the entertainment at the Ocean. This time I had a lovely companion to share the journey with and I was pleased I hadn't spent my time on the camps looking for someone I wanted to sleep with and had waited to find someone I wanted to wake up with!

We quickly found a small bungalow to rent just over the road from the Ocean, and settled in to enjoy our winter together. Jim and Lynda Noone were resident at the hotel and over the years we had become close friends. A think what is not widely known is that when Billy Butlin bought the hotel in 1953, the same company owned the Lido swimming pool at the bottom of the hill, Billy also wanted to buy that and build a monorail to run the guests back and forth from the hotel to the beach. Sadly, it was something the Brighton council wouldn't even consider!

One of the Redcoats Reg Seiger, was a talented painter. Reg was German, and although he spoke English well enough to be understood his knowledge of the language wasn't exactly perfect. On the walls around the ballroom bar were a number of excellent murals painted by the well-known Helen McKay RA, I had seen others painted by this gifted artist in bars at Filey. The General Manager of the hotel asked me if Reg could be spared to do a bit of touching up on the murals as some areas were getting a bit tatty. It was agreed and Reg spent some length of time doing this and did a first class job. Sometime later I was approached by him and he said he thought he should at least get some recognition for his work. He asked me if, in the corner of the wall, where she had signed "Helen McKay R.A" he could add "And Reg Seiger". I explained that to do that wouldn't be ethical as Helen was the original artist, however, I would agree that under her name he could add 'Touched up by Reg Seiger'. Reg was happy with this and for the next couple of years the sign became a private joke between the guests and the Redcoats, as on the wall was written "Helen McKay R.A touched up by Reg Seiger"

Marty and Peggy loved working at the Ocean and we had a very happy winter there. The following summer we returned to Pwllheli camp, taking Peggy with us. During this season Bill and his wife Sybil decided they wanted their second daughter Andrea, to be christened in the small church on the camp. They were friendly with Canon Pugh, and asked him to do the honours. Marty and I were asked to stand in as Godparents, and were delighted to do this.

Canon Pugh was a remarkable person and it was he who, in the late 1940s, had introduced the church to Butlins, and soon each camp had a church and a resident padre. He has appeared in a number of books written by former WW11 prisoners of war who had been captured by the Japanese and imprisoned in the notorious Changi Jail. Tom Pugh was the camp chaplain who, protesting at the cruelty to prisoners by the Japanese, marched out of the camp to report the matter to the Red Cross. The sentries were give the orders to shoot but Tom Pugh continued to march and did successfully report the matter.

In the days before emails messages were sent between camps via telex. At Margate I received one from a colleague on another site asking if I had any spare Harvest Festival hymn sheets. I hadn't and so contacted Canon Pugh's secretary, who didn't have any either and replied. " Canon Pugh has this in hand and will be supplying all sites." I telex'd a reply but the operator made a mistake and when the copy of my message came to my office it said "Canon Pugh has his in his hand and will be servicing all sites!" I found this to be very amusing, had it put in a frame and hung it behind my office desk. Canon Pugh, who had a wicked sense of humour, somehow heard about this and when visiting Margate came to my office and I saw him keenly looking at the wall behind my desk. When he spotted it he laughed and begged me to let him have it, which I did. He was a remarkable and amusing man.

That winter was spent at Margate and again Peggy was with us and, although we had no way of knowing at the time, the three of us would eventually do an unbelievable 18 years together. Peggy was an experienced Chief Hostess and she and Marty were a good team working together.

There were a number of advantages about working with experienced Redcoats in the hotels in the winter, one being that if you decided to put on a special or additional show, perhaps for Easter or Christmas, there wasn't a problem getting it on. Most of them knew all the standard Butlin shows or sketches. 'Old Time Music Hall', 'Maria Martin And The Red Barn Murder', 'The Minstrel Show', 'Western Night', most of us had played parts in some of them. It was usually just a question of deciding what to put on and it was my practice to let the Redcoats decide, have a meeting together and decide by a show of hands. If you happened to be running the show you had to be seen to be fair. If a couple of Redcoats missed being in the pantomime you made sure they were in the Redcoat Show or on the Cabaret. There was always a couple of the Reds who could do chopstick or limbo dancing and, coming from different camps, they all had their own version of party dances.

I thought of an idea that was very popular with the Margate and Brighton Redcoats and really enjoyed by the guests. I was entertainment manager of Margate and my counterpart at Brighton was Peter Millington. We had six very popular and capable acts at Margate and Peter had much the same situation at Brighton. I would put a film show on Tuesday evening and send my six acts to Brighton, a distance of 77 miles, they would travel in a Butlin vehicle. On Thursday, Brighton would send their six acts to Margate. On one night a week each hotel would have 12 good acts and six of them new to the guests. At Margate on Thursdays I put small tables all around the ballroom floor and left just a postage size dance floor. This was on the days when you could put candles in bottle for an intimate atmosphere. We had non-stop dancing and cabaret right throughout the evening from 8.00pm until midnight. Each of the acts did two short spots and the cabaret was interspersed with dancing. Peter did a similar programme at Brighton. Margate was self-contained with performers throughout the winter apart from Christmas and Easter when visiting acts were booked. Margate had a revue company throughout the summer performing in the Queens theatre. Brighton, didn't have a theatre and just had visiting acts for the summer when the ballroom became the theatre.

Marty and I always knew that one day we would be married and had on occasions discussed it. I think because we were together already, and with the sort of life we were leading, neither of us saw it as a pressing need. Often at the end of an evening we would feel the need for a walk in the fresh air and it would invariably lead to a stroll along the beach. We would, more often than not, finish up walking to The Captain Digby. On the way back one early morning we recalled our first walk there and I personally had always felt that was what had cemented our relationship. I remember stopping and telling Marty that I thought we should get married. We realised that neither of us had family in the area, Marty's family were in and around Bristol, and my family were further away still, and all around Yorkshire. Marty and I had been together for three years and were as close as we were ever going to be. If it was possible I loved her more than I had when we first met. Marriage would just be a formality as it had always been a foregone conclusion. We both decided that we wanted a quiet affair and agreed that we would keep it low-profile. In the end we went along to see the Registrar in Ramsgate and fixed a date. The only two guests we invited were the area manager Ron Hayter and his wife Anne. The whole thing seemed very brief and informal and was over in a couple of minutes. But it was just as official and binding for all that. It was certainly a quiet affair and, as I said to Marty at the time, if it had been any quieter it wouldn't have happened. I love her more today than I did then and it will be fifty years ago in January!

I was very impressed with one Redcoat in particular. He played to big laughs on the shows and was popular with the guests. A young comedian called Freddie Davies. He had been born with a tremendous asset for anyone in his line of work and his face could be described as 'a comic's dream'. He had the most expressive brown eyes and features that could be contorted into the most amazing comical expressions. As a result of this he was affectionately given the name "Parrot Face". I'd had a recent conversation with Liverpool agent Mike Hughes who had told me that he was on the lookout for young talented comedians. We phoned Mike from my office and he said that he had seen Freddie work and would guarantee him £40 a week for Freddie, then earning £14 a week, it must have seemed a fortune. That was the start of Freddie's amazing career which took him from the tough working men's clubs of the North East to the Royal Shakespeare Company. Seasons at the famous London Palladium with Cliff Richard, television shows with the legendary Judy Garland, touring the world with his stand-up comedy act and counting among his many fans the late film idol Cary Grant. Just another former Redcoat who would agree that Butlins was the greatest Springboard in the world for anyone with talent.

On one of his visits I had a long conversation with Colonel Brown, who said he felt I was ready for the hot seat of camp entertainment management and would be taking over this position at Bognor the for the coming season. I was thrilled and excited at the prospect and Marty was delighted. She mentioned it to Peggy who said she would love to join us, I was able to pull a few strings to arrange this. Entertainment Staff Recruitment for the forthcoming summer had started and I was asked to team up with Roy Markwell. Roy had been the manager of Bognor for the previous four years and had been promoted to area manager, overseeing Bognor and Minehead.

The system of recruiting staff for the entertainment department was quite simple. Applicants, in response to their letter of application, were sent an employment application form which they completed and returned to Head Office with a photograph. The forms were divided into area's right throughout the country. Applicants from Scotland would be interviewed at either Glasgow or Edinburgh and the application forms would be sent to the northern camp manager arranging the interviews. The interviews were conducted at Job Centres and often two or three Butlin entertainment managers would be interviewing in the same Job Centre at the same time. The manager interviewing would select the applicants he needed and the rest would be returned to Head Office to be placed in 'a pool'. I think an accurate estimation of the number employed would be in a ratio of around one in thirty. So, if you needed to replace 12 staff you would interview in the region of 350. The number of applications for jobs on the entertainment staff enabled you to be that selective. When I took control of four other departments I was shocked and appalled at the interview methods of some of the managers. Some interviewee's were dismissed after two or three minutes. I had to explain that each of them had written a letter applying for a job. In return they had received an application form, which had to be completed and returned with two references, together with a photograph. They had returned these and waited in anticipation for a number of weeks. Some had travelled a considerable distance to attend the interview and, after going to those lengths, must have felt shattered to be in and out of the interview room in two minutes!! I had to insist that every applicant was given at least 15 minutes.

Roy was to be based at Bognor, indeed, for the first couple of months we would be sharing an office but that wasn't a problem as Roy Markwell was one of the nicest men at Butlins. Not many staff were required and so I was 'inheriting' quite a number of Roy's staff from previous years.

I had a phone call from Bill Martin to tell me that Johnny O'Mahoney was under a bit of a cloud and going through a bad spell with the company. It appeared that a regular camper at Filey had given Johnny a ticket for the Wembley Cup Final, but on arriving there he had found a stranger sitting in the seat he had booked for Johnny. The stranger produced a ticket stub and said he bought the ticket from a dark haired Irishman in a pub! The regular camper complained to head Office and Johnny was told he couldn't return to Filey as the man who gave him the ticket was a regular visitor and there could be some embarrassment if he and Johnny were at Filey together. Johnny was foolishly banished to Mosney. I didn't agree with this and there could have been many reasons why Johnny had disposed of the ticket. Johnny had been put to work entertaining in Dan Lowrey's bar, but a big part of his personality and charm was in being Irish. In Dan Lowrey's bar he was just another Irishman!! After a few days he just packed and walked out. Wally Goodman had eventually traced him and he agreed to return but only if he could work with me. I accepted, of course, without the slightest hesitation. So Johnny would be joining us as Camp Comic for the summer and I was delighted at the prospect

Marty Chief Hostess, with Tommy Trinder, Skegness, 1965

Rocky & Marty with Bud Flannagan. Skegness. 1969

Chapter Sixteen

I WAS BACK BEHIND THE WHEEL OF MY CAR AGAIN but this time for the much shorter distance of just 72 miles to Bognor. On this trip I had two passengers, as Marty and I were taking Peggy with us. Bognor is a small camp and stands in just 60 acres, judging this against Filey's 400 will give some comparison. It is that size because, when Billy wanted to build at Bognor, that was the only land available for purchase. It has everything that the larger camps have but in some cases slightly smaller. It doesn't have a sports field for example and all the sporting activities take place on the Middle Green. Unlike other camps it could be said that Bognor camp is actually situated in the town. Handy for self-caterers and thrifty housewives who prefer to use the local shops. Like most of the Butlin sites it was conveniently placed for anyone wanting to do a bit of sightseeing, just a fifteen minute drive to Arundel with it's beautiful castle. The castle is a popular tourist attraction set in sweeping grounds and gardens. Just 22 miles along the coast in the opposite direction is the delightful coastal resort of Brighton.

I was most impressed by Roy Markwell's management skills and in particular by the way he handled the staff, he was firm but friendly and when he gave instructions he did it in a helpful and pleasant way. I had, for some length of time, realised that the method of dealing with staff in an entertainment department had to be quite different from that in most other industries. Especially when dealing with Redcoats. By nature of the job they had been engaged to do they were extroverts and encouraged to be. They were flamboyant but the job made them that way.

In my days as Chief Redcoat I had discovered that you got respect if you gave respect. The quickest way to lose it was by raising your voice, being belligerent or 'telling' instead of asking. Redcoats were outgoing, gregarious and flamboyant because that's what their job demanded of them. In a nutshell they were individuals and had to be treated as such. There was also a time, as I was soon to learn, that it was often prudent to 'look the other way'. The department had a lot of rules and some of them were rules that could easily be broken. By nature of their personality a Redcoat would occasionally break the rules but you didn't always have to see it - you could look the other way. In example if you knew that a couple of Redcoats had attended a late night rehearsal and left the theatre at two in the morning. The following day they had been on first sitting breakfast, and then had worked throughout the day and you spotted them that evening in a bar, hiding behind a pillar having a drink together, you didn't have to see them and could look the other way. I had a trainee assistant sent to me by Rank one season and he asked me *"Don't you ever take a late visit down the chalet lines to see what they are getting up to?"* I told him that I didn't have to spy on them down the chalet lines as I knew what they were getting up to! I could see that over a number of years Roy had built up a team who were loyal to him and good at the job they did. I adopted his policy and, at the end of the day, Peggy and I were together around 18 years, Sacha, the chief swimming coach perhaps 16 years. Paul Becket at Pwllheli and Filey was with us around 12 years.

George Humphries had been the Chief Redcoat at Bognor, when we teamed up together. Over the sixteen years or so we were in partnership he became assistant, deputy and then entertainment manager. In all the years Sacha and I were together we never had a fatality in the swimming pools.

Eric Winston, was a famous band leader and, of course, had an excellent band. Eric regularly broadcast around Europe from Butlins Bognor. My only problem with Eric was getting him on stage, or trying to. He would pass the baton to his deputy Roy Marsh, and spend most of the evening at the bar.

I suppose in fairness Eric's value was in the wonderful free publicity Butlins got from his broadcasts which went out all over great Britain and Europe. In any event he was a law unto himself, a major Butlin shareholder and a friend of Billy, Bobby and the Colonel so you couldn't win and Eric Winstone appeared on stage when he chose to.

The great Al Freid was the MD in the theatre, Al had played at the London Palladium and spent years with Moss Empires. Al fronted one of the genuine pit orchestras at Butlins. I recall just a few others who were real theatre orchestra's as opposed to dance orchestra's and there is a distinct difference. Ken McClean, at Skegness, who had also played on the Royal Yacht, and the excellent Paul Greaves, at Filey, and, of course, the brilliant Wayne Warlow, who later became Musical Director for BBC TV Cymru Wales, they each had 14 musicians. It was essential for musicians in the orchestra pit to be able, not only to sight read, but to transpose on sight. They were brought in when it was realised that the quality of performers at Butlins had outgrown the dance bands who were playing for them. Sadly it didn't last and due to cost Butlins had to revert back to dance orchestra's doubling the theatre. Having said that I must say he did it well!

Archie Craig was the stage manager at Bognor, and Archie was senior SM throughout the company. He was a very capable technician and, in the sad era of theatre closures up and down the country, he bought Rank Strand Grand Master lighting boards from theatres that had closed and installed them in the camps being built at Bognor, Minehead and Barry. He must have saved Butlins many thousands of pounds.

Johnny soon settled in and to see him and Peggy in full flight on the Sunday morning 'Campers Gathering' was a joy to watch. On the first Sunday the Redcoats just stood with open mouths, they had never seen anything like it. In my many years in the job and the hundreds of Redcoats, compere's and camp comic's I worked with I had never seen his equal and was never likely to. The 'Lucky Dip' audience participation show was Johnny's domain but at his request when, for whatever reason he hadn't been able to do it, I had done the show at Filey, and with his blessing I had used material I had seen him use many times. When I moved to Minehead and Pwllheli as deputy I was asked to present the show there. It was a great show and got good laughs but I always knew it was really Johnny's show and my show was a shadow of the one he did. He was doing the show at Bognor and also his balloon act in the Redcoat Show, other than that he had a roving commission and, working together with George The Chief Redcoat he did the events they both agreed on.

Marty and Peggy were sharing the responsibilities of Chief Hostess and it was working out very well. We had a good management team, Roy being area manager was the head of course, myself as entertainment manager, John Bennett, a very capable deputy and Roy Pellet, former leader of the Blue City Jazzmen was an assistant, we had an excellent team of Redcoats and the camp was running well.

Over the years it has become a well recorded fact that Butlins has always been regarded as a great springboard for talent. Bob Monkhouse who was known as "British Comedy's Golden Boy' and the finest stand-up comedian ever; one of the few performers who can be called a comedy-legend, gave me a quote for my book 'Gumshield to Greasepaint' here's what Bob said:-

'The greatest nursery for budding talent in the entire world has been the great network of Butlins Holiday Centres and Camps. As the variety theatre and seaside concert parties declined, Butlins provided the perfect training ground for fledgling singers and comedians instilling in them the realisation of the discipline and hard work required to survive in such a highly competitive business-as well as teaching them to live on thirty bob a week! Of course, for every Redcoat that winds up a star a thousand don't but every one of them had a chance to make it and so it's to the public benefit that only the best get to the top.

Signed,
Bob Monkhouse

Some of the greatest talents and biggest stars in this country got their start on a Butlin microphone and to name just a few:- Charlie Drake, Bill Maynard, Des O'Connor, Dave Allen, Clinton Ford, Jimmy Tarbuck, Russ Hamilton, Jimmy Cricket, Cliff Richard, Michael Barrymore, Ted Rogers, Mike Newman, Tony Peers, Colin Crompton, Mike Burton, Johnny Ball, Freddie 'Parrot Face' Davies, Terry Scott, Roy Hudd, Stephen Mulhern.

Talent however comes in many forms and when it's said that Butlins is a great launching pad for budding talent it doesn't necessarily mean a talent for treading the boards. I know for a fact that the 'Butlin Experience' has been used by men and women throughout their lives and their involvement has helped them to succeed in many different spheres and walks of life. I met such a person at Bognor, in the form of assistant manager John Bennett. John had an awesome appetite to learn, an incredible hunger to discover anything and everything about the entertainment business. His desire for this was contagious and I found myself enmeshed and wanting to help him. I sent John to spend an hour with Archie Craig, the stage manager and a former performer. He had an unusual talent for teaching newcomers and wannabe's the art of correctly using a microphone. There are a great many people who wrongly think they can use a microphone but they are simply using it like a telephone and speaking in a louder voice. Archie explained to his 'pupils' that a microphone is an instrument and, like all instruments, it has to be played correctly. Archie would explain, in simple terms, that inside the microphone is a thin membrane, known as a diaphragm and when sound waves strike the diaphragm they cause it to vibrate.

In technical parlance "When sound waves strike a microphone diaphragm, they cause it to move within an electro-magnetic field, which in turn, creates a variance in electric current. This signal is then transmitted to an output device - i.e. Speaker." In a nutshell Archie would show people that if you were to loud and too near you would create distortion, if you speak too quietly and are too far away you can't clearly be heard. Archie would stand at the rear of the theatre to listen to you and allow you to stand at the rear and listen to him. The result was - after a lesson with Archie you better understood the workings of a microphone.

John spent his entire life building and opening nightclubs and discotheques'. He DJ'd throughout Europe and, after an outstandingly successful career, made his living renting holiday villa's and apartments in Portugal and Spain. He would always attribute his success to the time he spent at Butlins. So, the camps weren't only a springboard for 'performing' talents!

Everyone settled in nicely and things were running well, however, in mid-season we experienced something totally unprecedented in the history of the company. It had never been done before and has never been repeated since.

The normal practice was to designate an entertainment manager to a particular camp. He would then recruit whatever staff was required, arrange the entertainment programme, produce a few shows and remain on that camp for the entire season. In fact it had always been customary for a manager to remain on a camp for a number of seasons. I was astonished to get a phone call from Colonel Brown asking if I would be prepared to move to Skegness, and saying he would be pleased if this could happen without delay. The Colonel explained that Marten Tiffen, who had been my manager at Filey and was now my opposite number at Skegness, was having personal family problems and as his home was in Seaford, just up the coast from Bognor, the move would be a big help to him. The Colonel asked me to think it over and ring him back. Marty and I discussed the transfer and, as we had no children or other responsibilities, we saw no why we shouldn't move. I phoned Marten, who briefly outlined his troubles and explained why it was important for him to be nearer home.

Marty and I had agreed to move essentially to help Tiff with his problems but, after I'd had time to think things over, I realised that Skegness was a much bigger camp and always considered to be one of the most important in the group. Under normal circumstances, it could have taken another three or four years before I was considered ready to manage Skegness! Marty and Peg' had become very close friends and Peggy asked to come with us and I was able to pull a few strings and arrange this. I tried to persuade Johnny to join us but he had made lots of friends and knew Marten from his Filey days and chose to stay. I was sad to leave him and would realise in years to come that no other person in my entire life had influenced and inspired me as much as Johnny Tynan O'Mahoney.

Chapter Seventeen

I was behind the wheel of my car again and the three of us were off on yet another exciting Butlin adventure. The excitement for Marty and Peg' was made even more so as neither had been to Skegness camp before- the camp that started it all. Smaller than Pwllheli camp, which the girls new so well, but, occupying two hundred acres much larger than Bognor with its modest sixty. Skegness could accommodate close to 10,000 holiday makers. Being the first venture by Billy Butlin into the then new and uncharted waters of holiday camps, the camp had deservedly earned its place in the hearts and minds of British holiday folklore. It was a wonderful camp-absolutely steeped in tradition and with many of the original buildings still standing and in use.

The Gaiety theatre was the most outstanding feature of the entire camp and the only 'real' commercial theatre on any Butlin camp. The chairlift running from the south side of the camp to the extremes of the north was the longest run in the Butlin Empire. Marty and I had no way of knowing, at that time, but Skegness would be our summer place for the next six years.

The Deputy Entertainment Manager, I inherited, at Skegness, was the very capable Jimmy Kennedy, who went on to have considerable success with Pontins Holiday's and, in a few years, would become their senior entertainment executive. Jim and I arranged to meet the first evening to 'do the rounds' together, doing the rounds was a term used for checking all the entertainment venues, which was done every evening starting with the first performance in the theatre at 5.30. It was essential that members of the management team did this important task to establish that events started on time and would run smoothly throughout the evening.

Walking to the theatre together Jimmy informed me that we had a rather worried assistant, who wasn't looking forward to renewing my acquaintance. This turned out to be Gus Britten, the lifeguard I had suspended for his unauthorized closure of the swimming pool at Margate. I smiled to myself as I recalled the Viking cartoon with the caption "Rocky Mason can kiss my arse!" When we arrived at the theatre I saw Gus standing in an aisle with his back to the wall waiting for the orchestra to start the overture. This was the cue for the theatre lights to be dimmed. When they were I quietly edged towards Gus and said "Drop your trousers Gus and let's get it over with!" He looked rather shocked but then looked at me and saw I was smiling. We shook hands and put the silly nonsense behind us.

My first season at Skegness was not a happy one. Entertainment management on a holiday camp is not an easy job. It starts with a visit to radio Butlin before first sitting breakfast to enable announcements to be made into the dining halls in the event of inclement weather. Rain would invariably lead to programme changes and the campers had to be advised. You would work throughout the day, mostly in the office, and the evenings would be occupied doing the rounds. In those years the average day would finish around midnight, a fourteen to sixteen hour day. Walking the camp a couple of times each evening, doing the coverage, could sometimes be a drag, especially when it was pouring with rain.

It could be pleasant and rewarding when you were checking the shows that you had produced yourself, or items in your own programme.

That first season I was checking someone else's shows, events and items that Marten had produced, and it gave me no real satisfaction. One thing in particular was causing me more than a little concern. Skegness like most other camps had two main ballrooms. One was regarded as the fun ballroom, where the Redcoats would feature party dances, square dancing, competitions and other entertaining items. At Skegness that was the Princes, it had a happy atmosphere and was running well. The other was the Queen's ballroom, and for serious dancers doing the waltzes, foxtrots and quicksteps.. With the advent of rock and roll, jive and disco, this type of ballroom dancing, from the majorities point of view, was on the decline.

The thing that caused me concern was the fact that this large, beautifully appointed venue, right in the heart of the camp had been taken over completely by no more than 30 serious dancers. They took over the entire room and spent the evening, on the floor, showing off their expertise. All the men wore shiny black, plastic dance shoes and the ladies silver, sequined ones. They were snooty and aloof and not your average Butlin campers. Jim confirmed that the same type of people came right throughout the season, with perhaps 30 or 40 occupying the dance floor and never more than 150 in the entire room and this had been happening for the past couple of years. I noticed that the Jimmy Symmonds orchestra, of fourteen musicians, were constantly propping up the bar and when I took Jimmy to task he said the dancers had told him they preferred to dance to their own records.

I checked the bar takings and found the bar was taking a modest £15 to £20 a night and no doubt most of that from the orchestra. I was determined to do something about it, but knew I had to be patient and make alterations the following season. To start altering things in my first few weeks would have been a slur on Marten's abilities. I had no choice but to sit on it until the end of season.

The winter was to be spent at Margate, and Peggy, Jim and his wife Eileen would be joining us. I had somehow assumed the job and title of senior compere and was now doing all three major competition's Northern, Southern and Grand Finals. The Northern Finals were held at Butlins Metropole, Blackpool, which was a nice break as Marty was always invited. Marty was a natural in the position of chief hostess, very attractive with a nice personality and never daunted. I was delighted to see her becoming very close to Daphne the wife of Colonel Brown.

I was never comfortable with the atmosphere at the Metropole and, in my opinion; this was due in no small measure to the general manager Mabel Warrell. Butlins had acquired Mabel with the hotel, she was the 'lady friend' of one of the directors Frank Barlow, and came as part and parcel. In my view she never wanted the hotel to be Butlins, and had her own way of running things. She had a beautiful suite of rooms, her food was provided and it was an open secret that she sent staff shopping for little 'specialties'. Mabel stayed on in her rooms even after retiring. With her lighting, heating and food and drink provided she had no living costs at all and it had been like that for 30 years! I wasn't surprised to be informed that dear Mabel died a millionaire.

I was having a drink with Wally Goodman and Maggie Lamonde, in the cocktail bar of the Metropole, when Wally casually remarked "Of course, you know I once owned the Metropole Rocky?"

I was stunned until Maggie burst out laughing and said "Yes, for two whole days you did!!" Wally then explained his story. One of the reasons Billy Butlin wanted the Metropole Hotel, was to see the name 'Butlins' on Blackpool's Golden Mile, but he was quite sure the local Council wouldn't. He also knew that if Billy Butlin was seen to be a potential purchaser the price could well be increased. Billy formed a property company, of which Wally became managing director, and Wally Goodman bought the Metropole Hotel!!

After a very pleasant winter, mainly spent at Margate, we returned to Skegness, and I had the opportunity to alter the situation in the Queen's Ballroom. The booking figures for the first few weeks of the season were in the region of 6,000, which didn't justify opening every venue. We were able to keep the Queen's Ballroom closed to effect a few changes.

Self-catering was quickly becoming our most popular type of holiday and more self-catering units were being built each year. This had resulted in the closure of a dining room, which gave me access to hundreds of unwanted tables and chairs. I had decided to transform the Queen's Ballroom into an enormous Cabaret Bar, and would present non-stop cabaret, interspersed with a little dancing throughout the evening. Tables with white linen table cloths were spread around the ballroom floor, and a small postage stamp sized dance area was left in front of the stage. During the first weeks of the season the bar's manager had saved the empty wine bottles, candles were put in the bottles and one placed on every table. When the lights in the room were dimmed low it gave a pleasant night club atmosphere. The printed entertainment programme was altered and the venue was re-named 'The Queen's Club Bar'. When we affected the alterations and introduced this new format, none of us knew it was the first step towards making the company many millions of pounds!!

I had a good feeling about the conversion and felt it would be right for the department but hadn't realised to what extent and how enormously successful it would become. It was only with hindsight that I realised that the majority of bookings for Skegness were drawn from northern towns, the very birthplace of Working Men's Clubs! The new Club Bar would give them the entertainment and atmosphere they enjoyed and were familiar with. There was had no budget for providing entertainment in the new venue and, for the first few weeks until the venue was established, we had to really scrimp. Redcoats were used who were in the Redcoat Show, but doing different acts, those who were not quite good enough were also used. Acts were purloined from the talent show, and the odd session available from the revue company artists. In short, anyone who could entertain was given a chance and we were able to use a few acts from the staff welfare show.

The venue was an enormous success from the very start, we saw the audience build up on the first Saturday evening to, in the region of, 1,200. My mind boggled when I saw the bar takings, an unbelievable £240! Doesn't sound much at today's prices, but we have to realise that at that time a pint of beer was, in old money 11 pence a pint. At today's prices that was less than 5p! At the time it was a rare event to get a bar taking that amount of money.

I was delighted when we sustained those kind of takings throughout the week. Suddenly the venture was the talk of the company and Colonel Brown and Wally came to visit. When asked the Colonel didn't hesitate and immediately authorised the booking of visiting acts. This was done through Len Norton's, Sheffield Agency. We couldn't afford to bring acts in to cover the entire 3 hours each evening. We brought in 2 acts nightly and continued with our existing practice. Each visiting act did two spots and so it enabled us to be more selective with the others.

It had always been Butlin policy to stop the entertainment and bar service and close the bars at 11.o'clock. Indeed, a tradition called 'Penny On The Drum' was started for just that purpose. A team of Redcoats would parade in a line around the bar singing the old Salvation Army number 'Who'll put a penny on the drum', encouraging the campers to join them. They would then all march in line to the ballroom and the bar had been cleared. But a great deal of progress had been made since that was started in the late 1940s. An idea was going round in my head and the more I thought about it the more I began to like it. I decided to approach Colonel Brown about trying an experiment in the Queen's Club Bar. The idea was to close the bar as usual at 11.o'clock, have a quick clean-up of the floor and tables and re-open at Midnight. Making a small admission charge would pay for a suitable three act bill. The show could go on until 2.30 am. and would also be an opportunity for the guests to have a late night drink. To my amazement, without any hesitation, the Colonel approved and asked Wally to arrange it with me.

After we had spoken about it Wally booked Freddie 'Parrot Face' Davies, who was doing a season on the local pier, Hughie Green, with Monica Rose and Yvonne Marsh, who were performing at the Arcadia theatre in town. It had been decided that a buffet would be included and we would charge 10 shillings (50p) The show was 'plugged' over Radio Butlin, throughout the weekend and tickets went on sale on Monday morning and were sold out in 2 hours!

Bobby Butlin, Colonel Brown and Wally Goodman came to see the show which was extremely well received, there was a great atmosphere and the room was buzzing. Hughie Green, Monica Rose and Freddie Davies were popular TV personalities at the time but now, perhaps for the first time, the audience were seeing them live, they liked it and showed it with applause. At the end of the show an appeal was made for peace and quiet as they returned to their chalets. The following morning Bobby, the Colonel and Wally held an inquest and everyone agreed that the evening had been an absolute and total success; the only small adverse comment was made by the Colonel who hadn't liked people queuing for the buffet. I must be honest and admit that I only saw it as a means of making money after midnight when the bar would normally have been closed. Colonel Brown, in his wisdom, had a far broader vision and said "What took place last night means far more to us than just a bit of revenue in a bar after midnight. It has been established that we can put on entertainment after midnight, but more important we've proved that we can make a cover charge for admission. By doing that we can now book any act in the country. The modest charge that was made last night more than covered the cost of the artists and the musicians overtime. Not only can we book the best acts in the country, but we can advertise that fact to bring in bookings!"

The following season it was presented on two nights a week on all the camps under the banner of 'Big Night Out'. Head Office later did a survey and it was found that ticket sales averaged a thousand in each venue for every performance. Bar takings established the average drink sales was three drinks per customer, chicken baskets had been introduced and were waiter served to avoid queuing and an average of 700 chicken baskets were sold each evening. Although it ran for at least twenty years to my knowledge I would say, as far as presentation was concerned, its pinnacle was when we had a fourteen piece orchestra on stage and the full complement of revue dancers. To see twelve girls in gorgeous plumes was something very special. It wasn't long before Show Bars were being built on all the camps, especially for Big Night Out.

Some of the artistes booked: Late Night Cabaret

Ken Dodd, Bob Monkhouse, Lulu, Ted Rogers, Harry Worth, Vince Hill, Ray Fell, Diana Dors, The Baron Knights, Russ Abbott and The Black Abbotts, Frankie Vaughan, The Batchelors. Bernard Manning, Charlie Williams, Norman Vaughan, Larry Grayson, Frankie Howard,

Mike Reid, Jim Davidson, George Roper, Mike & Bernie Winters, Matt Monro, Leslie Crowther, Norman Collier, Bernie Clifton, Brothers Lee, Nicky Martyn, Hope & Keen, Johnny Hackett. Bert Weedon, Ronnie Dukes & Ricky Lee, Warren Mitchell, Faith Brown, Frank Ifield, Beverley Sisters, Joe 'Piano' Henderson, Lenny Bennett, Tom O'Connor, Roger De Courcey and Nookie Bear, Hughie Green & Monica Rose, Tommy Cooper, Dick Emery, Don McClean, Shane Ritchie, Brian Conley, Lenny Henry, Tom O'Connor, Joe Longthorne, Duncan Norvelle, Pat Mooney, Bob Carolgees, Freddie 'Parrot Face' Davies, Jimmy Marshall, Les Dennis, Freddie & The Dreamers, Frank Carson, Stu Francis, Bobby Davro, Roy Castle, Lenny Henry.

In those days, most camps had two ballrooms and as ballroom dancing had begun to wane the venue's started to be used for midnight cabaret. They were hardly suitable and it wasn't long before the company began to build attractive showbars which were far better for the type of show we were presenting. Late Night Cabaret literally made £millions for the company and the figures below would have been the takings if we had been doing it in the present day, which is comparable to the days we were doing it.

A pint of beer at Butlins is now £3.45 and so, if we take that as the average price of a drink. The 1,000 attending averaged 3 drinks per person.

3000 @ £3.45	£10,350.
700 chicken baskets @ £7.50	£5.250
	£15.600
Two nights a week x 2	£31, 200
18 weeks season	£561.600
On 9 camps	£5054. 400

Chapter Eighteen

IT IS A WELL RECORDED FACT THAT BILLY BUTLIN raised millions of pounds for a number of charities and it has been said that he could never say 'no' to a worthy cause. He is reputed to have given in the region of £5 million pounds from his own pocket. Sir James Carreras, Past President Variety International, said of him:

"Billy Butlin was one of the most human beings I have ever met. He was pleasant and nice whether things were going well or badly. He was a man concerned about people. He cared about them. There are very few who cared as much as he did. You cannot talk about Billy Butlin the man or Billy Butlin the benefactor. There was no difference between them."

He then told the story of how someone had brought to the attention of the Variety Club, the case of a young girl who was blind, deaf and dumb. Billy started a trust fund for life for that girl and she is still living in hospital with wonderful medical care in a special wing he financed. Billy Butlin was one of the biggest supporters of the Variety Club's Sunshine Coaches projects, this came about after a visit to a hospital to see a special therapy swimming pool for handicapped children donated by the Variety Club. The matron took him into a room where a number of severely handicapped children were strapped into wheel chairs.

"These children", she said *"have a life expectancy of ten years, and none of them have been outside this hospital."* When asked *"Why is that?"* She replied *"Because we have no vehicle that can accommodate their wheelchairs."* Billy bought the very first Sunshine Coach and eventually provided another 47 costing in all more than £200,000-the largest number bought by anyone in the world.

He gave more than £2000,000 to various Variety Club charities, including £250,000 for an EMI brain-scanner for the Great Ormond Street Hospital. Not only was he a generous benefactor to the numerous Variety Club charities, but he used the Butlin Empire to also support the Duke of Edinburgh's Award Scheme, and the National Playing Fields Association. The full extent of his charity commitments no one will ever know. What is known, however, is that his kindness has made life happier and given health and hope to untold thousands of children all over the world. Despite-or perhaps because of- his humble beginnings and the building of a mammoth holiday empire which made him an international celebrity, he has always remained a man of humility and charm. Always sensitive to the feelings of others, deeply concerned with the welfare of the sick, the disabled and less fortunate.

With Billy Butlins services to the Church, providing a resident chaplain on all the camps and a visiting chaplain arranging services at the hotels, coupled with his enormous contributions to diverse charities, it was inevitable that his efforts would ultimately be seen and justly rewarded. This happened in 1964, when Billy was summoned to Buckingham Palace to be knighted by the Queen. Sir Billy described it in his own words:

"It was a most impressive ceremony. After being ushered forward by a series of imposing-looking officials I finally entered the Ballroom, where the Investiture was held, and knelt before her Majesty, who touched me on the shoulder with a sword. 'Do you wish to be called Sir William or Sir Billy?' she asked, smiling. I replied: "I have always been called Bill or Billy, your Majesty". .. "Very well," she said. "Arise Sir Billy"

Sir Billy's decision to retire from the company was taken very suddenly and as a result of what appeared to be extremely punitive taxes being imposed on the wealthy. Denis Healey, Chancellor of the Exchequer, in a famous television interview said *"I shall squeeze the rich until the pips squeak! We shall increase income tax on the better off and I warn you there will be howls of anguish from the rich."* Britain's tax regime was one of the most punitive in the world and triggered an exodus of entrepreneurs and highly paid stars such as David Bowie, who went to live in Switzerland, and the Rolling Stones, who left for the South of France. These penal rates were imposed on high earners during the 1968 economic crisis. It meant a person with an investment income of more than £6,000 would pay tax of 20 shillings and nine pence - or £1.04 today - for every £1 of income, while someone with an investment income of above £15,000 would pay total taxes of 27 shillings and three pence -or £1.36p on every pound. In his own words Sir Billy says:

"My accountant told me that I would have to pay a "one off" special charge and including income tax and surtax I would be paying 27s 3d on every pound of my income - in those days there were 20 shillings to a pound. To put it mildly I was stunned. It would mean paying £30,000 more than my total income. The only way I could pay this huge bill was to sell a large chunk of Butlin shares. (At today's rate £30,000 would be £429,300.)

There was talk in some quarters of still more punitive taxes on the wealthy. There was also talk of taxing donations to charity and if that happened it would have made it impossible for Sir Billy to continue to help the charities that depended on him. Sir Billy reluctantly reached the conclusion that the case for leaving Britain for a tax haven was overwhelming. He chose Jersey in the Channel Islands. The Daily Express published the following comment.

"Sir Billy Butlins decision to quit Britain for jersey because of tax burden is a most unhappy one. Few Countries-least of all Britain which relies so heavily on the talents of her people - can spare men of such outstanding ability. Yet, as Sir Billy says, why, after giving £2,000,000 to charity, should he hand the rest of his fortune to the Exchequer?"

Of the early days of his retirement Sir Billy says: *"I missed Butlins, I missed being involved in the company's business. When I first retired I became a consultant to the company-but nobody consulted me. Bobby was 34 when he took over the business. He had been in it for fourteen years and obviously had different ideas from me on how it should be run and taken into the future. I must admit that I was angry when he started making changes and didn't consult me. When I look back now I realize it was natural for Bobby to want to do things his way and I must admit he has proved himself an excellent businessman".*

Leaving Britain was a terrible decision for Sir Billy to make. It had been his home for most of his life, where he had created a major business and Britain was where most of his friends lived. Sir Billy and the company had paid more than £50 million in taxes and in return he was now faced with a five day deadline and had to go before the end of the financial year on April 5th 1968.

He had been told by his accountant that he must resign his position with Butlins and relinquish any other directorships and business interests in Britain. He had to transfer every single asset to Jersey before April 5th. He had to put their home Windlesham Moor on the market and remove all his personal possessions. That must have been a terrible wrench for both of them. It must be said that he made a determined effort at 'retiring' in Jersey and stepped up still further his work for various charities. He personally took charge of landscaping the grounds of their new home. When Sir Billy bought the house it had a field with one tree adjoining it. He planted 100 apple trees, forty flowering cherry trees, several thousand rose bushes, rhododendrons and camellias. He had dozens of peacocks strutting the lawns and typical of him he bought 600 budgerigars, which flew freely over the island, returning to their nests at night. He tried to remain busy and active but, gradually, the full impact of retirement began to hit him. The camps had been his whole life seven-days-a-week and 24 hours a day.

He had remained with Butlins as an unpaid consultant but the truth was Bobby didn't need him. At first Sir Billy had been angry when Bobby never consulted him about company affairs. But, suddenly, he began to realise, wasn't this what he had trained Bobby for, why he had been put to work in various departments, why he had gone to Stowe? He recalled how, when Bobby was an officer cadet, he had dissuaded him from joining his friends and going into the guards. He had instead joined the catering corps where experience in large-scale catering would stand him in good stead when he joined his father on the camps. Bobby, of course, also had a point of view.

"He says he was angry after he retired at not being consulted on the running of the business. I knew he was hurt, but I had to do things the way I felt was right and that meant cutting myself off from him. I could not go through with the charade of consulting him and then totally ignoring his views. That would have upset him even more.

It took a threat from an outside source to heal any rift there might have been between them. Phonographic Equipment, a firm that supplied gambling machines and had acquired ten per cent of Butlin shares attempted a takeover. Sir Billy and Bobby joined forces to oppose the merger. Both strongly believed that an organization connected with gambling was not suited to run Butlins which has always been a business catering for families. Butlins have always had bingo, and penny fruit machines, and filmed horse racing was introduced in the late fifties, but there was a big difference between those and actual gambling machines. They both wanted Butlins to remain a family holiday and not have gambling machines on the camps. Some of these machines can accept stakes of up to £100 and have been called the "crack cocaine" of gambling. They won their battle and the rift was healed.

Chapter Nineteen

THE SOUTHERN CAMPS, NAMELY BOGNOR, CLACTON, MINEHEAD AND BARRY were being run as Winter Social Clubs, with facilities contained in a particular building or area of the camp. The club at Bognor had incurred a loss of £620 over the past two winters. (£620 at today's rate would be £9,300).

On one of his visits Wally had told me that I was returning to Bognor, during, the closed season, as general manger of the social club. Marty and I were pleased for a number of reasons: we had found Bognor to be a lovely area and a nice place to spend the winter, and Marty had recently given me the news that I was about to become a father! Bognor would be ideal for this as there was an abundance of holiday flats in nice areas.

We didn't have far to look as, on our arrival, we discovered the company had arranged a lovely flat in Canning Court, Felpham. It was within 45 ft. of the sea and almost on the beach. We lost no time in booking Marty into the Zachary Merton Maternity Hospital, and I can't think of a nicer place for a couple to have a child. It was a lovely hospital with the friendliest of staff, and in what seemed no time at all we were rushing Marty in there where she presented me with our most beautiful daughter Sam. Our daughter's name wasn't meant to be Sam, if she had a been a boy we might have called her Sam, which is perhaps a good name for a bloke. We spent hours discussing what might be the most suitable name and eventually agreed on Samantha. But when we were holding the little thing in our arms Samantha didn't seem affectionate enough somehow. It got shortened to Sammy. Later in life it became just Sam-and it stuck!

A meeting had been held with everyone who had worked in the Winter Social Club over the past couple of years. A bit of research had told me that those using it had been paying a nominal membership fee for the entire winter and then had free admission to the club. At the meeting, the staff told me that the members refused to pay the few pence to use the cloakroom facilities and just put their coats over the backs of chairs. The club had been open seven nights a week and each night had been a mix of old time, modern and sequence dancing to organ and drums. But the majority just seemed to regard it as background music as they formed themselves into groups to play cards. The bar staff complained that they hardly served a drink but, looking round the room most people were drinking. It seemed the practice was to buy one drink to obtain a glass and then refill from handbags. I asked who ran the heated indoor pool and was told it was never busy enough to merit a lifeguard and most nights nobody used it at all. I wondered if they couldn't justify a lifeguard's part time wages how could they justify spending £43 a week (£615 today) heating it? There was obviously a great deal wrong and 'things' had been allowed to slide. It all needed a good shake up.

We put a stop to heating the pool and had it emptied and locks put on the door. Some of the managers pointed out that when we got planning permission to build the camp it had been agreed with the Council that we would provide swimming facilities and so we made the necessary arrangements and laid on a mini cab to take any swimmers to Chichester Baths. (it was never used) The club was opened on just three nights a week and guests paid admission at the door. Wednesday night was Old Time and Modern Sequence to a trio playing organ, bass and drums.

We gradually built up to an attendance of 250 to 275 which was an acceptable number. Friday night was for youngsters and for our opening night we put on Gino Washington and the Ram Jam Band, who had two of the biggest selling UK albums of the 1960s. The second week we had Jimmy James and the Vagabonds. Young people in Bognor had never seen anything like it and flocked to the club. We had also posted flyers and leaflets at the naval base at Portsmouth. The end result was an attendance of around 1,250 a night and we had no less than sixteen floor walkers. Saturday night was a real shocker for the staid residents of Bognor-Regis. We had brought down Sheila Mc Cale a vocalist from Skegness, in the position of Club Hostess. We booked two more acts usually a comedian and a male vocalist. But also booked two further acts from 'Pop Parker'. Whilst not exactly strippers they were exotic dancers who almost stripped and known in the business as 'Tit & Bum'. Most acts would do two spots nightly and so it was virtually a non-stop cabaret evening interspersed with a bit of dancing. We opened at 8.0'clock and closed at Midnight and played to around 1,000 every Saturday. Needless to say the debt was cleared in a matter of weeks.

We moved back to Skegness for the summer season and, now that we had our baby daughter the general manager Harry Oaks, kindly arranged for us to have a furnished flat in the Ingoldmells Hotel. It's well known that Skegness camp became HMS Royal Arthur, a naval training camp, during the Second World War. What the young sailors suffered sleeping four to a chalet, with no form of heating whatever, in the grim conditions of a freezing Skegness winter beggars the imagination.

The camp padre Cliff Malkinson, told me of a dreadful tragedy that had occurred during the camps naval days, when four young seamen had tried to get some warmth one freezing night by drilling holes in an oil drum to make a form of brazier and burning coke as fuel. There had been a build up of deadly toxic fumes in the night and the lads had been found dead in the morning. The victims of that dreadful incident are buried in the churchyard of St Peter and Paul, in Ingoldmells, and Cliff took me to see the graves and their small military headstones.

One of the stalwarts of the entertainment department at Skegness, was the most famous Butlin children's uncle of them all, the legendary 'Uncle Boko'. Who, wearing his trade mark fez, entertained children at the Skegness camp for over 20 years. He proudly boasted that he was entertaining the children- of- children he had entertained in his early years. He was an excellent ventriloquist and magician who was absolutely devoted to his job. He didn't smoke, never drank and would never even be seen in a bar. Boko, whose real name was Frank Keep, lived in a chalet on the camp with his lovely wife Elizabeth, who was a Redcoat house chairman.

Uncle Boko was an enormous help to Anne Hayter, the founder of the famous Butlin Beaver Club in 1951. The Beaver Club was started for campers children who were under the age of 9 years old. There was a grand initiation ceremony for new Beavers which was performed by King Beaver aka Uncle Boko. Within the first couple of seasons the Beaver Club, which was featured on all the camps, was boasting over 200,000 members. Membership was for life and Beavers received a badge, a Beaver money box, and every Christmas and birthday a Beaver card. I will truly never know how Anne Hayter, managed to do this. I visited her frequently in her Beaver Lodge, as she called it, in our Oxford Street, Head Office.

It was from here that the birthday and Christmas card were dispatched. All the Beaver Enrolment Cards were kept in a number of filing cabinets lined up against the walls. In those days, before computers became almost mandatory, everything had to be written by hand. Anne Hayter and just two assistants managed to keep on top of this. Every Beaver was told the secret password which must never be divulged, but children were also taught that they must never tell lies or keep things from their parents. Therefore, the secret password was 'Buzz Off', so, if a parent or anyone asked the child to divulge the password - they were told 'Buzz Off'. So they hadn't been guilty of telling a lie!!

THE BEAVER CLUB RULES:-
Be kind to dumb animals.
Eager always to help others.
Aim to be clean, neat and tidy.
Victory by fair play.
Energetic at work and play.
Respect for parents and elders.

THE BEAVERS SONG
If you're a Butlin Beaver you're a friend of mine,
If you've the Beaver Spirit then the world is fine,
In our lodge you'll find good company,
To be a Butlin Beaver is great fun you'll soon agree.
We are the eager Beavers and we promise true,
To keep the golden rule in everything we do.
Come and join us-wear a badge-learn the secret sign,
Be an Eager Beaver-Busy Eager Beaver-
If you're a Butlin Beaver you're a friend of mine.

Sadly Uncle Boko passed away in his chalet in 1968, and it was the saddest day I have ever known on any Butlin camp. Not only were the Redcoats heartbroken but so were other members of the staff, the campers and children. God bless you Uncle Boko, you were a legend RIP.

With Roy Castle and Bobby Butlin, Filey 1983

. 'The Management Team 1983' L to R. Ron Stanway. John Wilson. Alan Ridgeway. Dave Moore. Brett Cresswell. Red Brigden. Eamonn Andrews. Rocky. Ken Idle. Frank Mansell. Bill Haydon. Doug McLoud. Wilfred Orange.

Chapter Twenty

WE RETURNED TO BRIGHTON FOR THE WINTER but the arrival of our lovely daughter meant that quite a few things had to change; we had now become a family and Marty felt that it was time to settle and have a permanent base. Some weeks before we had spent an evening with Colonel Brown and his wife Daphne.

Marty told me that she had taken the opportunity to discuss with Daphne our desire to settle and buy our own home. A few weeks after our return I had a phone call from the Colonel, and he suggested that I should take Marty to have a look at High Lodge. Some years ago I had lived there with half a dozen other Redcoats, and so I knew the house well, it was a big, beautiful, imposing Tudor style, detached property with black timber facings on white skimmed walls. It had large split level gardens and as soon as Marty saw the house it was love at first sight.

The Colonel told me to have the house valued and to get the valuer to send him the valuation in writing. I contacted a local agent who put the value at £6,200, which was sent to the Colonel. We contacted building societies and made arrangements for a mortgage on that figure. The Colonel phoned me a few days later and I was astonished when he told me he had spoken to Sir Billy, and I was to put in a bid for £4,000. We were delighted to see that over a third had been knocked off the actual valuation. Our guess was that it was yet another 'thank you' for my efforts on midnight cabaret! To put it in the right perspective; if High Lodge was valued at £600,000 in today's money that enormous discount would be £200,000!! Thank you Colonel Brown and Sir Billy Butlin.

Jimmy Noon, the talented keyboard player, was still at the Ocean with his wife Lynda, they would ultimately spend 30 years there and a total of 40 with the company. Jimmy, who had spent a couple of years at the Blackpool Metropole, told me he was delighted that the former catering manager there was coming to the Ocean as general manager, his name was Rod Rodgers, a big affable man with a warm and generous personality. He quickly established himself as an excellent general manager. During the few weeks before Christmas when the hotel was quieter than usual he organised large Christmas parties with enormous success. One of the most successful was the Brighton

Cleansing Department Christmas Ball.

Rod and I worked well together, became firm friends and formed a friendship that would last for 50 years. Rod very soon became area general manager of the entire hotel group, and was a very significant figure in the purchase of the Grand Hotel Group, which included The Grand Hotel Scarborough. A most imposing hotel overlooking the towns South Bay. When the hotel was built in 1867 it was one of the largest hotels in the world. The building is designed around the theme of time: four towers to represent the seasons, 12 floors for the months of the year, 52 chimneys for the weeks and 365 bedrooms to symbolise the days of the year. It was bought by Butlins in 1978. Rod was also active in the purchase of The Grand Hotel Llandudno, with 168 en-suite bedrooms and situated on Llandudno's North Shore, offering spectacular views out over the bay.

The hotel was acquired by Butlins in 1981 and in 1998 Butlins sold off all the Grand Hotel Group to 'Grand Hotels Ltd', the managing director of which was a certain Rod Rogers!

After six wonderful years at Skegness, we were delighted to be told that we would be returning to Pwllheli in North Wales. We were pleased for a number of reasons, Pwllheli is a beautiful part of the world and a nice place to live also it was regarded as a promotion. There was a form of 'pecking order' with entertainment managers. The company seemed to start managers on the smaller camps and when they had gained experience they were moved to larger ones. Barry, Bognor, Mosney and Ayr were considered to be smaller camps. Then in some form of order, it seemed to be Clacton, Minehead, Skegness and then Pwllheli. Filey was always regarded as 'the flagship of the fleet'. A managers salary and hospitality allowance was reflected in the size of the camp. The allowance was actually called "Reciprocal Hospitality Allowance" and was to enable the manager to buy drinks at the bar for visitors and artistes.

The move was a stroke of good fortune in other respects as it enabled us to lease out High Lodge at a good rental. Also it had been agreed by the company that managers with families could remain at their camp and not have to move to hotels for the winter. I had a family now and could exercise that right. Marty, Sam and I could now have a permanent home, but more than that- house prices in North Wales were far cheaper than in the South of England!! The company had arranged for us to have a self-catering chalet. We were pleased to see there hadn't been too many changes and soon had the camp up and running. Sam had grown out of the baby stage and was in a push chair and loved to go for walks to feed the ducks on the boating lake. Sam has always been the original Butlin babe, born 'just over the fence' from the camp at Bognor, and living her early years at the Ocean, Bognor, Skegness and now Pwllheli. Sam would eventually spend the first 15 years of her life on one or the other Butlin camps and hotels and there's no prize for guessing what her first job would be! Yes, she became a Redcoat at Brighton, Minehead and Blackpool.

Peggy asked to join us in our move, together with Sacha Van Weenen, the chief lifeguard also Gordon London, a very good GD Redcoat. It was the beginnings of an excellent team and they would all go on to see years of Butlin service. Shortly after our arrival Marty told me she had been struggling on the car park with boxes of shopping and with Sam in her pushchair, when she was approached by a young man who asked if he could help. He had no idea who Marty was but, chatting as they walked to the chalet, he told her he worked on the skating rink and his name was Paul. He said his biggest ambition in life was to be a Redcoat. I got to know Paul over the next couple of weeks and discovered he was, as Marty had described, a very friendly and nice young man. I invited him to the office for a chat. We quickly found a replacement for him on the rink and he became a GD Redcoat. Within three or four seasons he was chief Redcoat, after moving to Filey with us he became a compere. Eventually Paul Beckett became entertainment manager of Minehead and had a 37 year career with the company.

Towards the end of the season we started house hunting and eventually found a delightful bungalow on a private estate on the road to Abersoch and this was to be our home for the next five years. Whilst waiting for the contract to be signed, despite the camp being closed, we stayed on in the chalet.

At night, when it had fallen dark, Sam loved to sit on my lap in our car and 'drive the car' down to the sports field which would be swarming with rabbits. There were literally hundreds of them. We would 'freeze' them in the headlights and Sam would then dip them and sound the horn, she would then shriek with delight, to see dozens of them disappear in seconds. Pwllheli was a lovely place to live and there was so much to see on car trips throughout the winter and we tried to have a picnic most weekends. Our favourite area for this was

Snowdonia, we found the scenery breathtaking and discovered some beautiful places.

There was nothing glamorous about working on a holiday camp that was closed for the winter, in fact it was quite the opposite. I had been given no brief and was never told what to do, but of course, you had to keep yourself justifiably occupied. One of the assistants who lived locally had asked me about the possibility of finding him a job for the winter and had explained how difficult it was to find work in that part of Wales. I had already gone through the paper work for previous years and seen that quite a number of jobs had been put out to contract and knew that doing these jobs would more than justify his wages. I had already planned a winter works list.

The boating lake came under the umbrella of the entertainment department and painting the 18 rowing boats would save hundreds of pounds which had in the past been paid to a contractor. That would be the first assignment. The acts and musicians had always complained that the stage in the Regency Bar was too small and now there was an opportunity to enlarge it, also building a 'walk out' ramp for the stage in the Spanish Bar would be a big improvement. I was useful with tools and would be able to join in on those jobs as being retained on a camp that was closed for the winter meant you had to be 'down to earth' and prepared to get your hands dirty now and then. For quite a number of weeks after the 'close down' there was a great deal of admin work to be done. Colonel Brown always insisted on a full End Of Season Report covering every aspect of the department. There was a system for grading every visiting and resident act, band, group and musician. A full staff report was submitted, indicating individuals who were suitable for Butlin events in their particular area or attending show jumping and pony club games at Wembley. Staff were graded as to their suitability for future employment, information that would be very useful to a successor if a manager left or was moved on.

Later on there would be a couple of Entertainment Managers Conferences to attend and these were usually a three day event held at Head Office in Oxford Street. When February came around I would be travelling the country with Frank Mansell, auditioning acts for the coming season. Shortly after this, with the other entertainment managers, I would be visiting major towns throughout the country attending staff interviews. When I returned from those I would be virtually tied to the office preparing and planning for the season.

Chapter Twenty One

IT WAS AROUND THIS TIME THAT BUTLINS DECLINE in the holiday market started to increase and become even more noticeable. Cheap package tours abroad had been on the market for a number of years. In fact the Horizon Holiday Group had pioneered the first foreign package holiday as early as 1950 with charter flights between Gatwick and the then not very popular destination of Corsica.

By the late 1950s and 1960s, these cheap package holidays- which combined flight, transfers and accommodation- provided the first chance for most people in the United Kingdom to have affordable travel abroad. In the late 1960s and early 1970s several major tour operators started doing very cheap package deals and opening up mass tourism to mainland Spain, the Spanish islands, Greece and the Greek islands, Italy and Portugal's Algarve. It was realised of course in the 1960s that this type of holiday was having a marked effect on all British holidays and Butlins was simply experiencing the problems of the British seaside holiday market in general.

The company sent teams to all these destinations to check the strength of the competition as far as prices were concerned. The results were not very pleasing and they all came back with receipts for the purchase of food, drink and other everyday essentials and all of them showing the items were far cheaper abroad than at Butlins. I suppose it was only to be expected that these countries who were trying to market tourism, which was a complete new product, would sell their product cheaply to make it as attractive as possible. Indeed, the product was so cheap and competition between tour operators so intense that it lead to the collapse of several major travel companies.

In August 1974 Horizon and Clarksons both collapsed leaving 50,000 tourists trapped abroad and a further 100,000 facing the loss of booking deposits. There were a number of reasons why many of our regular customers stayed with us. They were happy with the product we had to offer. Many had never been abroad and found the prospect a bit daunting. A number had never before been on an aircraft and were averse to flying. A great many stayed with us but not in the required numbers and Butlins started to feel the pinch and the need to cut back on spending. There are a number of examples of this, our orchestras were reduced in numbers and came down from 14 musicians to just 8.

Very soon some of the bands started to disappear altogether the theatre orchestras were amongst the first to go and the ballroom bands started doubling and playing for the shows. The revue dancers were also reduced from 12 girls to just eight. The roofs of the chalets and the main buildings had always been painted on a rotation system with each roof being painted every three years, but now roof painting became less frequent.

Other aspects of maintenance were also reduced and the camps started to show signs of neglect. The roof situation became more obvious when taking a ride on the chairlift or monorail. Butlin camps weren't the only branch of the market to feel the pinch. It affected other camps, hotels and seaside boarding houses.

Cheap, package holidays were not the only reason for the decline in bookings for Butlin holidays, there were a number of other reasons as well.

There had been considerable changes in the needs of British holiday makers in the three decades from the middle of the 1940s, to the mid-1970s. In the early years, just after the war, the majority of the British public weren't used to taking annual holidays, and when they did they regarded themselves as being fortunate just to be on holiday and weren't too demanding on standards. Few people in those early days had cars and so their choice of holiday was more limited. By the mid-sixties most families had cars, and the introduction of television had, to some extent, given them more sophistication. The British public had begun to appreciate and demand higher standards when on their holidays. Butlins had to start investing, particularly on accommodation, to reach these new expectations.

That is the situation the company had found itself in when I was asked to move back to Filey.

We had enjoyed four very pleasant years at Pwllheli but I was thrilled at the thought of returning to Filey as, being my first camp, it held some very fond and special memories. Over the years I had been lucky in acquiring an excellent team of staff. Sacha, the chief swimming coach had started with us at Skegness and moved with us to Pwllheli, and was now coming to join us at Filey. Liam Kelly, the bar host and guitar vocalist was also coming. Gordon London had also been with us from Skegness, and was also joining us. George Humphries who had started with us as chief Redcoat at Bognor and was now deputy manager, was also coming, together with Paul Beckett, the chief

Redcoat, Chris and Kathy and of course dear Peggy Warner.

Shortly before we left Pwllheli I was summoned by Bobby Butlin to a meeting at head office to be informed by him that the company was going to be re-structured and, as a step towards this I was being given a different role. I couldn't believe my ears as my new responsibilities were reeled off by him. My new title would be Leisure & Amenities Controller and as such I would continue to be responsible for the running of the entertainment department, but my new management role would also embrace the licensed bars, the shops, kiosks and retail outlets together with the coffee bars. I would also be responsible for the amusement park, children's playground, chairlift, gaming arcades and even the train rides around the boating lake and to the beach! In short every leisure and amenity on Filey centre. I was delighted of course and couldn't wait to get started.

Fortunately the move didn't take place for a few weeks and that gave me the opportunity to give a great deal of thought to the restructuring situation at Filey and what it would mean to the management team. I knew and respected the fact that most of the managers had been with their departments quite a number of years. Derek Hullah, the licensed bars manager had, just like me, worked his way through the ranks for some 25 years, the same applied to Dick Cappleman and John Bowen, who ran the retail shops. Also, I knew that Doreen Nattrass, the manager of the coffee bars had been with Butlins far longer than any of us, in fact Doreen was in charge of coffee bars when I had joined the company. I had, in effect, worked for Alf and John, collecting waste paper on the amusement Park and I was quite aware of how difficult things could be if they were not approached in a sensitive and sensible manner. The first vital step would be to assure everyone that their position of seniority and their management roles would not be diminished in any way and I was determined this would be done.

Chapter Twenty Two

I COULDN'T BEGIN TO DESCRIBE THE ENORMOUS FEELING OF JOY that I felt driving through the gates of Filey, after being away for so many years, remembering and reliving the magic of that very first time. The memories came flooding back and I saw ghosts waiting to welcome me at every turn. Big Alan Hayward and Harry Griver were waving in the distance, Patsy stood on a corner and blew a kiss. Johnny O'Mahoney was here, there, and everywhere.

I recalled the pride I felt the first time I wore the red and whites, a feeling vanity which only be measured by the vain gloriousness of being made chief redcoat. I realised of course, as I relived those moments of utter bliss, that things had changed. I was no longer that young carefree spirit, devoid of responsibility. In those for off days I only had myself to think about, but now I was married, with a wife and daughter. I also had the responsibility of running almost the entire camp. Things in my personal life had changed but I was pleased that not a lot had changed on the camp and the changes that had been made were all enormous improvements.

One excellent new venue was the Showbar for the late night cabaret show, it had seating for over 1,000 customers, an excellent sound system, and good stage lighting. The stage was adorned with beautiful drapes and I could see it was a bar that would be a pleasure to perform in. The former Regency ballroom had been converted into an enormous club bar. There hadn't been many structural alterations and tables and chairs had simply been spread over the large dance floor as we had done at Skegness. Liam would quickly settle in and make the Regency his own domain.

I was well aware on becoming involved with departments that for years had been run, and I have to say most efficiently by experienced managers, that I would have to take great care not to ruffle anyone's feathers. The first step towards this, as I saw it, was to assure them that there would be no attempt in any way to take over the running of their particular department. There would be absolutely no loss of face to them and they would not in any way lose any management control of their staff or department. My main concern was how to get this point over to them. I eventually decided that it would be better to speak to each manager individually. I set about doing this and the first person I saw was Derek Hullah, the licensed bars manager, he was the most senior manager amongst them and ran the largest department. I felt that if I could win Derek over the rest would quickly follow. Derek, like the rest of them, had more knowledge of his department in his little finger than I had in my entire body and I started off our meeting by telling him that! It didn't take much to win Derek over.

We had known each other for many years and he placed his trust in me. I simply told him the truth and that I had no intention of acting like some superior executive and trying to run everything like a one-man-band. I was also delighted to get the total support of the others. The offices for each department were spread over the length and breadth of the camp and my first objective was to get everyone under the same roof. We achieved that quite easily. The old photographic department went back to the very early years, when the guests didn't own cameras. 'Butlin Photographic', as it was called, had over the years fallen by the wayside.

Almost every family who came these days had at least one camera of sorts and had no need to purchase holiday souvenir photo's. This had made the photographic department almost defunct. The old photographic department building was almost in the centre of the camp and above all the various rooms were under one roof. We quickly set about converting them to offices and we all willingly and happily did the work ourselves. I had very quickly realised that one good thing about having all the departments under a 'Leisure & Amenities' banner meant that if Bobby or anyone else in head office wanted figures or information they only had to speak to one man. They didn't have to phone half a dozen different departments. The system had to be altered slightly and this simply meant engaging a computer operator to work nights. Before going off duty at the end of the evening each department would furnish this operator with takings in the various venues. These would be collated in a master ledger and the information would be available for anyone wanting it, or wanting to discuss a situation, the following morning. It also enables all of us to see, in an 'open book' situation exactly the way things were going. The department became an enormous success but not because of any brilliant management technique on my part it became successful because of everyone's sensible co-operation.

As the next few seasons came and went I would look back over the years and reflect on my thoughts and impressions when walking through the gates of Filey for that very first time. . I had somehow come full circle and the pleasure I had had over the years was far more than I ever expected. The success I had enjoyed went far beyond my wildest dreams and I must admit to the vanity of feeling quite proud of what I had achieved. But it must be said however that nothing could equal the sheer joy and total elation I experienced at making Chief Redcoat. That for me was one of the happiest and greatest moments of my long career.

There is a mystery of an old painting from Filey camp which I have never been able to get to the bottom of. The painting was in a religious theme and was hanging on a wall in the foyer of the camp church for many years. It was taken down by Jim Batten, a manager on the maintenance department, on at least two occasions, washed with soapy water. The foyer of the chapel was never locked and was open to the public night and day. I saw the picture being taken into the strong room of the cashiers department and enquired as to what was going on. I found it hard to believe when I was told that some sort of art expert had been on the camp, seen the painting and told the general manager that it could be a work of art.

I was later shown a copy of the Sunday Times newspaper which claimed that Sir Alec Martin, chairman and senior picture auctioneer at Christie's, secretly sold paintings, including Dyce's "Lamentation of Christ", to Sir Billy in 1941. The paper said Sir Billy, who was said never to pay more than 50 guineas for a painting, transferred them to his holiday camp company at a profit. They were then written down against tax and sold back to him. One of the paintings is said to answer the description of "The Lamentation of Christ" by William Dyce (1806 - 1864). Dyce is classed as a highly important pre-Raphaelite painter. It could also be the work of the Italian artist Parmigiano (1503 - 1540) or the Italian Francesco Trevisani (1656-1746). Mr Christian Weston said "We are extremely excited to be instructed by Butlins, if of course, the picture is correctly attributed to any of these artists, and it will be a most important art discovery". I made numerous enquiries over the years but was unable to discover anything further and the reason for my interest is "The Lamentations of Christ" is thought to be worth between £250, 000 and £500,000.

Perhaps, because of my long service with the company, being the same age group and having a mutual love for Butlins, I became close friends with Bobby. I also spent quite a bit of time in the company of Sir Billy during my 30 years on the camps and in the hotels. Early in my career he would want to know about the boxing in the New Sports Stadium.

Later, when I was Chief Redcoat, he would speak to me about Redcoat activities and I would spend time with him when he came with his entourage on his tours of inspection. Later, of course, as an executive, I would find myself in his presence in a variety of situations. Whatever position I found myself assuming in the company I was always enthralled by this remarkable man and was unashamedly proud to work for him. In the many years that I was with him I heard lots of stories and witnessed for myself a number of amusing little anecdotes that only serve to establish the playful, often childish and wicked sense of humour that was a part of this wonderful man's persona.

On Clacton camp one Saturday, the intake day, he saw an elderly lady sitting next to a gentleman in a corner of the large reception with their suitcases at their feet. Passing through again sometime later he was surprised and concerned to see them still sitting there. Sir Billy spoke to a receptionist who explained the camp was completely full and there wasn't a chalet available. The elderly couple had arrived without a reservation and were waiting in the hope of an unlikely cancellation. Sir Billy told the receptionist to give the couple his chalet and he would make other arrangements. A few days later he saw the old lady sitting by the swimming pool and asked if she was enjoying herself. She said *"Mr Butlin, I am having a wonderful holiday but can you find out the name of the old man you have put me in the chalet with?"*

Three sides of the Marine Bar in the Butlins Ocean Hotel, Brighton contained enormous glass fish tanks that covered the entire walls. They were about 50 feet long and 10 feet high. Drinkers in the bar would watch the many thousands of exotic, shimmering, dancing goldfish darting hither and thither. On one of his visits Sir Billy looked in a litterbin at the entrance to the bar and saw a dead goldfish.

Apparently, a member of staff had seen that one of the fish was dead and had disposed of it. Sir Billy went into the bar to join the managers for a drink. He stood drinking with the general manager for a short while and then stepped towards one of the fish tanks. After studying it intently for a few moments, and watching thousands of glimmering darting goldfish, he turned to the general manager, and asked *"Who feeds and takes care of the fish?"* The general manager, looking a bit confused, gave him a name and Billy said *"Well keep your eye on him, there's one missing!"*

Most sadly, at 3.30 in the afternoon of Thursday 12 June 1980, Sir Billy Butlin the Extraordinary Showman, Holiday Camp 'King' and remarkable philanthropist passed away. His death would not only be an irreplaceable loss to his camps and the millions who used them but to the entire country if not the world. The great man was laid to rest in St John's cemetery on the island of Jersey. Standing on Sir Billy's grave is a large edifice weighing eight tons and measuring four feet high and ten feet wide, made of Scandinavian stone and costing £80,000. The memorial has elaborate carvings depicting scenes from Sir Billy's life and inscriptions which trace his years; a camp scene with swimming pool and chalets, an amusement park and the jolly fisherman who appeared on the famous Skegness poster. His wife designed the monolithic edifice personally. Shortly after the great man's funeral, I was enormously proud when Bobby asked me to be an usher at his memorial service at St Martin's-in-the-Field, London.

What a fitting occasion it was with the church packed with celebrities from every walk of life and almost every star in show business coming to pay their respects.

Colonel Brown said in his address to the packed congregation:

"Bill was a combination of two characters the super showman, the brash opportunist, at times ruthless in the pursuit of objectives, and just one layer under the tough exterior the quiet nature-loving, humble, self-effacing loyal friend, whoever sought to do good by stealth."

The Colonel finished his address.

It gives me comfort to dwell upon
Remembered friends who are dead and gone,
And the jokes we had and the fun.
How happy they are I cannot know
But happy am I who loved them so.

Noel Coward

Perhaps that is the right note on which to end my book and this tribute to Sir Billy Butlin a most remarkable gentleman.

May I thank you Sir Billy for those thirty most wonderful years. Sleep well Sir, God bless you and rest in peace.

The main responsibility for entertaining the guests and keeping them happy fell to a body of hand picked men and women whose origins go back to 1936 and the opening of Skegness, the first Butlin camp – The Famous Butlin Redcoats.' To list all those who were privileged to wear the coveted red and white uniform would take several books. Here is a selection

REDCOAT ROLL OF HONOUR

Shireem Abraham. Jack Acers. Steve 'Grizzly' Adams. Neil Ainsby. Stuart Ainslie. Wendy Albinston. Kim Aldridge. Cliff Alger. Maeve Allan. Dave Allen. Len Allen. Sandra Allies. Julie Catchpole-Allinson. Lesley Allsopp. Marion Amos. Emma Amriding. Andy Anderson. Bob Anderson. Richard Apps. Mick Armetidge. Chris Armstrong. Ken Arnold. Shane Ashe. Derek Ashton. Jennie Austin. Andy Ayliffe. 'Shakin' Dave' Atkin. Fabia Ali Kahn.

Archie Baker. Dave Baker. Wayne Baldwin. Johnny Ball. Simon Barker. Bob Barras. Frankie Barry. Helen 'Hels Bels' Barton. Kay Basano. Hillary Bateman. Mark Bates. Paul Baxter. Phillis Bayley. Angus Beadie. Robert Beaton. Suzie Beaton. Dannie Beattie. Michelle Beatty. Paul Beckett. Lin Bedell. Patsy Bell. Tom Bell. Drew Bennett. Kim Bennett. Ray Bennett. Kay Berry. Maggie Billington. Roger Billington. Anthony Bilton. Andy Birkmyre. Elaine Bishop. Melanie Blakeborough. Sarah Bloomfield. Peter Bolton. Cappy Bond. Colin Bonney. Karen Bonutto. Alan Booth. Allan Booth. Chris Booth. Vanessa Boother. Irene Boult. Toni-Jayne Bouncer. Selwyn Bowen. Ally Bowley. Dot 'scotty dotty' Boyle. Maurice Boyle. Joe Boyle. Laury Boynton. Sandra Bradbury. Norman Bradford. Libby Bradshaw. Dave Brady. Mandy Brady. Stan Branson. Pete Brayham. Norman Bremner. Ricky Brent. Pat Bridle. Red Brigden. Sue Briggs. David Bright. Pauline Bright. Barney De Brit. Barry Britten. Debbie Britten. Gus Britten. Paul Brocklebank. Les Brooks. Deanna Brookes. Hal Brookes. Sheila Broughton. Bob Brown. Jackie Brown. Jacqui Lidgard-Brown. Stephen Brown. Terry Brown. Tommy Brown. Vy Brown. Wally Brown. Pat Brownhill. Jo Brownlee. Charlie Bruce. Leo Buckley. Frankie Bull. Nigel 'slime' Burgess. Andy Burke. Richard Burke. Pat Burke. Sharon Burke. Norman Burns. Jean Burrell. Mike Burton. Nick Butler. Dave Butler. Paula Butterfield. 'Big' Joe Byrne. Lee Byrne. Dee Bance. Kerry Brimecombe. Andy Bidwell. Jan Byles. Sheila Burdon. Vicky Bailey. Peter Blow

Dave Caffey. Larry Cahart. Gemma Cahill. Kevin Caine. Dave Cairns. Val Calder. Ian Campbell. Kevin Campbell. Sheila Campbell. Cappy Carpenter. Jane Carfoot. Helen Carlow. Marie Carr. Rob Carson. Bill Carter. Stan Carter. Dave Case. David Casey. George Casselton. Pat Cawley. Paul Cawley. Karen Chalkley. Rosemary

Challoner. Danielle Chamberlain. Albert 'Sham' Chambers. Val Chambers. Dawson Chance. Chris Chapman. Sarah Chapman. Roy Charles. Huvre Charmwood. Jimmy Charters. Wendy Cherry. Al Chinnery. Jack Clancey. Margo Clancey. Brain Clark. Carol Clark. Colin Clark. Jenny Clark. Karine Clark. Kim Clark. Laura Clark. Mike Clark. Tracie Clark. Beverley Clarke. George Clarke. Mike Clarke. Norah Clarke. Geoff Clegg. Alan Clements. Averil Clements. Rachael Cleverley. Steve Close. Fiona Cockburn. Alison Cole. Jeanette Coleman. Martin Coleman. Mandy Collard. Alison Collier. David 'Tony C' Collier. Cliff Colson. Maggie Compton. Alex Connell. Kay Connell. Cathy Conner. Kathy Connors. Christine Chester. Bill Conroy. Rusty Constadine. Don Cook. Jackie Cook. Lesley Cook. William Cooke. Carole Cooper. Harvey Cooper. John Cooper. Julie Cooper. Andrew Cope. Kev Copeland. Cozzie Cosgrove. Colleen Cotton. Tom Cousins. Dave Cowap. Dave Cox. Lorna Cox. Norman Cox. Paul Cox. Sarah Cox. Terry Cox. Brian Coxhead. Susan Cranny. Brenda Cresswell. Brett Cresswell. Maggie Cridge. Karen Marsden-Croft. Roger Caldwell. Melanie Cross. Ted Crozier. Callum Cunningham. Robin Currell. Deanne Curtis. Tony Carney. Sue Clare. Dee Coles. Martin Coleman. Stephen Callary. Sue Clare. Penny Corner. Daniel Conroy.

Beryl Dale. Terry Dale. Bob Daley. Ian Dall. Reginald Daniel. Dorothy Daniels. Kelvin Davey. Freddy 'Parrot Face' Davies. Martyn Davies. Philip Davies. Russell Rees-Davies. Frankie Day. Kevin Deacon. Al Dean. Pat Dean. Rachel 'Cantrill' Dean. Vince Dean. Paul Delaney. Pat Demano. Vince Demano. Alex Dempsey. Alister Denholm. Brian 'Jockey' Denholm. Patricia Denny. Shirley Denton. Kevin Devane. Andy Diamond. Kim Dickins. Deborah Dixon. Bill Dodd. Hillary Dodd. Maureen Dolling. Phil Donaghue. Sandra Donaghue. Donna Donnelly. Marie Donnelly. Peter Donohue. Jordan Doolan. Lois Doran. Roy Doran. Cheryl Dow. Alan (A.B.) Downie. Danny Downing. Phil Doyle. Charlie Drake. Mac Draycott. David Drewitt. Flo Dukes. Danielle Duncan. Linda Dunn. Maggie Dunn. Babs Durkan. Johnny Durkan. Ralph Durkan. Mike Dwyer. Angie Dymott (nee Kelly). Rob 'Robbo' Dymott. Jack Davies. Steve Davies.

Graham Eagland. Robbie Eastcott. Richard Ede. Elizabeth Edwards. John Edwards. Les Edwards. Sandy Edwards. Stan Edwards. Keith Ellam. Brian Elliot. Graham Elliott. Mary Elliot. Jean Emmett. Andrew Emmott. Sue Emmott. Kevin English. Gareth Evans. Wayne Evans. Kaz English. Dave Fairhurst. Martin Fairs. Pam Fears. Yvette Featherstone. Christine Field. Stuart Field. Tony 'Zippy' Filer. Dave Fish. Kim Fisher. Michael Fisher. Sheila Fitzgerald. Mike Fitzpatrick. Kelly Flaherty. Leila Flannagan. Irene Fletcher. Paul Andrew Flinders. Marc Flint. Hazel Flynn. Kathy Flynn. Ron Flynn. Clinton Ford. Dicky Ford. Jackie Ford. Carl Foster. Joanne Foster. Charlie Fowler. Charlie Fowles. Dave Fox. Ian Frazer. Sue Frazer. Leon 'Lee' Freedman. Brian Freeman. Johnny French. Tamie French. Colin

Fretwell. Ken Frost. Mary Frost. Roger Fry. Ian Fullerton. John Furnoux. Valery Flower. Anne Gaghan. Mollie Geary. Robin Gee. Terry Gee. Mark Gee. Steve Gibbons. Derek 'Vic' Gibson. Paul Henry Gilbert. Nick Gilchrist. Melanie Giles. Stella Ging. Les Glass. Yvonne Glass. Mark Glassett. Audrey Glen. Peter Glen. Shaun Glenwright. Tommy Godfrey. Beth Goldie. Richard Gooch. Steve 'Goodie' Goodfellow. Anne Goodwin (now Yates). Neville Goodwin. Pat Goodwin. Paddy Gorman. Christine Gould. Lisa Goulding. Harry Gower. Lou Grant. Louie Grant. Terry Grant. Helena Bobby Green. Vic Green. Sally Greenfield. Harry Greenslade. Charlie Grey. Ami Bowsher-Grief. Andy Griffen. Gerry Griffen. Felicity Griffiths. Mike Griffiths. Steve Griffiths. Harry Griver. Mike Grogan. Brian Groves. Ian Groves. Anne Guppy. Chris Grey. Dennis Hackett. Tony Hacon. Bob Hadlow. Simon Hall. Kay Hamilton. Russ Hamilton. Allan Hampton. Darren Hannaford. Muriel Handley. Scott Handley. Stephen 'Worzel' Hanlon. Pam Hardman. Trevor 'Tinsell' Harland. Paula Harper. Al Harris. Brian Harris. Doreen Harris. 'Professor' Johnny Harris. Lyn Harris. Wendy Harris. Lee Deano Harrison. Joe Haskin. Bob Hastings. Matt Hattrick. Adrian Haughton. Graham Hawkins. Bobby Hayes. Chris Hayes. Neil 'Howie' Hayward. Johnny Haywood. Graham Heath. Danny Hegan. Maureen Heggie. Leah Helmsley. Sue Henwood. Averil Herbert. Terry Herbert. John Hewitt. Lesley Hey. Gordon Hill. Barry Hills. Heather Hills. Monique Hindle. Andrea Hines. David Hines. Colin Hitchin. Bev Hoey. Alan Holden. Craig Hollingsworth. Leanne 'Skippy' Hollis. Paul Holmes. Roy Holmes. Jo Holroyd. Stewart Hoof. Judy Hope. Ken Hopson. Roger Horniblow. Sandra Horniblow (nee Bradbury). Ann Hough. Ian Hough. Kathy Houghton. Johnny Hubble. Roy Hudd. Mark Hudson. Doreen Hughes. Ted Hughes. Bev Humphries. George Humphries. Sian Humphries. Ronnie Hunter. Vikki Hunter. Steve Huntley. Stuart Hurley. Jackie Hutchinson. John Hall. Kim Higgins. Ken Idle. Mavis Idle. John Igoe. Clare Ingram. Jimmy Ingram. Steuart Kingsley-Inness. Peter Lee James. Roger James. Steve James. Margaret Jay. Craig Jefferson. Noel Jeffrey. Billy 'Scouse' Jellyman. Val Jellyman. Michelle Davies-Jenkins. Mike Jenkins. Irish Jesson. Paddy Jesson. Barry St John. Mark Johns. Tracy Johns. Don Johnson. Martyn Keast. Eddie Keene. Alan Kehoe. Sharon 'Kelly' Kelleher. Martin Kelleher. Angela Kelly. Liam Kelly. Tony (Junior) Kelly. Biddy Kempster. Jane Kempster. Eileen Kennedy. Jimmy Kennedy. Michelle Kennedy. Shaun Kennedy. Chris Kenny. Dave Kessle. Alan Kettleborough. Liz Kildare. Tommy Killgallon. Andy King. Brian King. Paula King. Scott King. Mable Kingston. Stephen Kirk. Marian 'Kiwi' Kneale. Larry Knight. Bert Knott. Johnny Knott. Laura Kate. Peter Lacey. Lorraine Lamb. Jane Lang. Colin Langmead. Joy Larson. Kenneth Larson. Jax Lavery. Johnny Lawrence. Stevie Lea. Eddie Leather. Dave Lee. Frankie 'Plonk' Lee. Jan Lee. Tina 'Kirky' Lee. Valerie Leopard. Al Lever. Philip Lewis. Thelma Lewis. Peter Linstead. Gordon

London. Hayley Long. Paul Long. Holly Longman. Frank Lord. David Lowe. Teddy Lowe. Kevin Lumb. Dave Lyall. Alex Lyness-Brown. Larraine Lamb. Josephine Leary. Alison Leary. David Lynne. Jim Lord. Sammie Murton. Scott Macarthy. Sheila Mackenzie. Tracey Madel. Martin Maggs. Kathy Maher. Paula Manchester. Johnny Manns. Dizzie Mansell. Maria Mansfield. Ron Manville. Terry Manville. Roy Markwell. Shaun Marsh. Gary Marshall. Gordon Marshall. Jack Marshall. Bill Martin. Val Martin. Carol Martin. Chris Martin. Kim Martin. Mike Martin. Ray Martin. Alec Mason. Daz Mason. Geoff Mason. Jan Mason. Marty Mason. Rocky Mason. Sam Mason. Carl Massey. Ian Mather. Debbie Mathers. Brian Mathews. Helga Mathews. Monika Mathews. Terry DeMaxim. Gerry Peter Lacey. Lorraine Lamb. Jane Lang. Colin Langmead. Joy Larson. Kenneth Larson. Jax Lavery. Johnny Lawrence. Stevie Lea. Eddie Leather. Dave Lee. Frankie 'Plonk' Lee. Jan Lee. Tina 'Kirky' Lee. Valerie Leopard. Al Lever. Philip Lewis. Thelma Lewis. Peter Linstead. Gordon London. Hayley Long. Paul Long. Holly Longman. Frank Lord. David Lowe. Teddy Lowe. Kevin Lumb. Dave Lyall. Alex Lyness-Brown. Larraine Lamb. Josephine Leary. Alison Leary. David Lynne. Jim Lord. Sammie Murton. Scott Macarthy. Sheila Mackenzie. Tracey Madel. Martin Maggs. Kathy Maher. Paula Manchester. Johnny Manns. Dizzie Mansell. Maria Mansfield. Ron Manville. Terry Manville. Roy Markwell. Shaun Marsh. Gary Marshall. Gordon Marshall. Jack Marshall. Bill Martin. Val Martin. Carol Martin. Chris Martin. Kim Martin. Mike Martin. Ray Martin. Alec Mason. Daz Mason. Geoff Mason. Jan Mason. Marty Mason. Rocky Mason. Sam Mason. Carl Massey. Ian Mather. Debbie Mathers. Brian Mathews. Helga Mathews. Monika Mathews. Terry DeMaxim. Gerry Maxim. Ron Maxwell. Alan Maynard. Bill Maynard. Alan McBride. Ricky McCabe. Tony McCauley. Ruth McCulloch. Kay McDowell. Sean McGarry. Alex McGowan. Ann McGreevy. Frank McGroarty. Wendy McGroarty. Jackie McIntyre. Lisa McKinley. Maggie McMath. Michelle Meacher. Peachy Meade. Leslie Melville. Duncan Menzies. Mamie Menzies. Johnny Merrick. Brian Merritt. Shirley Merritt. Phil Merry. Lynn Metcalfe. Tony Middleton. Steve Middlewright. Dusty Miller. Kathy Miller. Tracy Miller. Joanne Millington. Peter Millington. Geof Mitchell. Gordon Mitchell. Julie Mitchell. Mary Mitchell. Phil Monks. Adam Moore. Dave Moore. Martyn Moore. Terri Moore. Patricia Moorhouse. Jojo Moreschi. John Morgan. William 'Bill' Moriarty. Alex Morris. Lynn Morris. Babs Morrison. Ray Moseley. Gillian Moss. Colin Mould. Carl Moulding. Martin De Mullen. Jason Mulvey. Brian Mundell. Tony Murphy. Danny 'Dee' Murtagh. Dave Muscroft. Tam Maguire. Debra Mathews. Kerry Miles. Judy McBearty. Gary Marshall. Chris Morley. Trevor Metcalf. Marion Medhurst. Shelly Naughton. Brian Nelson. Sue Nelson. Ronda Newell. Hayley Newman. Mike Newman. Alan Nicholls. Mark Nicholls. Pricilla Nightingale. Johnny Nock. Jimmy Noone. Ken North. Dave

Norton. Sandy Norton. Shane Norwood. Anne O'Brien. Des O'Connor. Phyllis O'Connor. Trish O'Hara. Olive O'Keele. Johnny O'Mahoney. Pat O'Malley. Jude O'Neil. Paul 'Oggie' Ogden. Carl Oliver. Mike Onions. Barbara Orange. Phil Orbell. Helen Organ. Jason Orme. Alison Orr. George Outram. Glynis Outram. Des Owen. Maire Owen. Steve Ogden. Johnny O'DonnaghueAl Page. Bob Paine. Tony Parker. Marsha Parton. Colin Patterson. Colin Paxton. Joyce Pay. Tony Peers. Elizabeth Penfold. Bryn Peters. Dawn Phillips. Andy Phillpot. Linda Pickup. Diane Pigott. Wally Pigott. Carol Pinkney. Adam Pocock. Anne Pooles. Stave Pope. Alan Powe. Robin Poulter. Michael Joseph Pratt. Bob Price. Gordon Price. Richard Prior. John Proctor. Heather Pullan. Denise Porter. Jaqui Rafferty. Joe Rafter. Shirley Rashbrook. Ted Ravenhill. Lin Read. Jack Reed. Jacki Rand. Jacqueline Reed. Eddie Rice. Frank Richards. Mollie Richards. Molly Richardson. Ray Richardson. Roly Richardson. David Rickus. Susan Rickus. Alan Ridgeway. Marj Ridgeway. Arthur Ridings. Dawn Ritchie. Dave Roberts. Jean Roberts. Roger Roberts. Neil Robertson. Mike Robins. Johno Robinson. Martin Robinson. John Roctor. Sarah Roddick. Alan Rogers. Jason Roper. Henri Rouah. Vicky Round. Helen Rowe. Jojo Savage. Wayne Savage. Pete Scally. Billy Scott. Suzie Scott. Paul Selby. Jaki Severns. Clare Seymoor. Doreen Shaw. Joe Shaw. Dave Sheard. Sue Shenton. Paul Sheppard. Tracey Shield. David Shires. David Naughton-Shires. Tanya Simons. Dave Simpson. Tina Simpson. Sid Sims. Janet Sinclair. Anita Singer. Rod Skinner. Carol Skuse. Wayne Slater. Bill Smales. Alan Smith. Christina 'Bonnie' Smith. Claire Louise Smith. Jimmy Smith. Karen Smith. Marg Smith. Mathew Smith. Maureen Smythe. Mick Smythe. Donna Speake. Roger Squires. Debbie Stahl. Julie Stallard. Keith Standed. Ron Stanway. Sharon Staples. Warren 'Mr Magic' Starling. Billy Stenson. Roy Stephens. Dave 'Shakin' Stevens. Dave Stevenson. Bill Stewart. Mornie Stewart. William B Stewart. Pat Stewart. Gail Storey. Les Stott. Kelly Stringwell. Nigel Stuart. Karen Sugarman. Stan Sullivan. Ian Summers. Tony Sweet. Karen Sugarman. Kevin Salter. Sue Smith. Steve Smith. Dawn Strout. Steven Antony Swain. Gerry Sexton. Lee Simpson.Alan Tait. Jimmy Tarbuck. Joe Taylor. Kelly Taylor. Ken Taylor. Kevin Taylor. Lisa Pricilla Dawn Taylor. Lucy Teal. Bill Tennick. Marge Tennick. 'Aunty' Sue Thistlewood. Annie Thomas. Beian Thomas. Dave Thomas. Wayne Thomas. Bobby Thompson. Graham Thompson. Ron Thompson. Valentin 'Lord' Thynne. Johnny Timpany. Karen Titchmarsh. Steve 'JohnBoy' Tobin. Anna Traynor. Frank Tremarco. Monika Mathews-Tresidder. Julie Trimble. Donna Turner. Sarah Tuson. Alyson Twiddy. Somon Tyler. Kim Tyrell. Sharon Thurman. Johnny Johnny Tait PaulaTanswell. Chris Tarrant. Clare Underwood. Trevor Upton. Johnny Van Earl. Jason Van Weenen. Sacha Van Weenen.

Dennis Venton. Sue Vernon. Andrew Mat Vilenko. Toni Vitti. Karen

Vertigans.

Marge Waddingham. Marge Waddington. Maggie Waldren. Mat Walker. Tony Walker. Mathew Walker. Eddie Wallace. Elizabeth 'Little Liz' Walsh. Alexa Walters. Brian Ward. Mike Ward. Carol Warner. Peggy Warner. Valda Warwick. Brian Watson. Mally Watson. Arthur Watt. Jacquie Waugh. Bob Webb. Chris Webster. Mark 'Macker' Weightman. Sandra Wells. Brian West. Rod Wheelwright. David White. Su White. Tracie White. Brian Whittle. Frankie Whittle. Roy Wicks. Valda Wicks. Chrissie Wiggins. Harry Wilks. Claire Williams. Jack Williams. Paul Williams. Pete Williams. Phil Williams. Clifford Willingale. Jan Wilson. John Wilson. Ronda Wilson. Sandy Wilson. Stewart Wilson. Valerie Wilson. Dean Winter. Jo Winter. Terry Winter. Jean Winters. Sonnia De Witt. Alan Leslie Wood. Amanda Wood. Debbie Wood. Doris Wood. Ken Wood. 'Big' Phil Wood. Susie Woodard. Reg Woodley. Elaine Woolsey. Francis Worrall. Willie Wright. Derek Woodward. Kirsty Woodward. Gill Wooderson.

Jerry Yardley. Alfie Young. Anne Young.

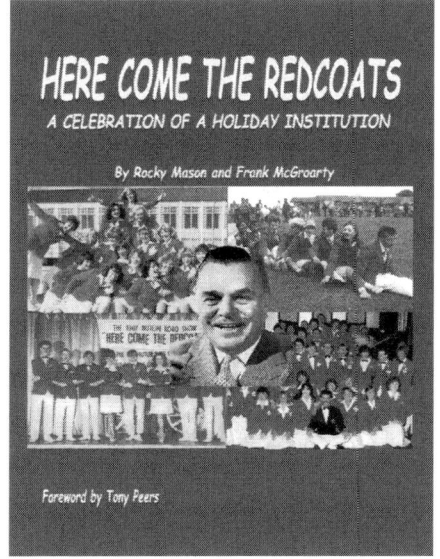

Both published by Authorhouse UK

Printed in Great Britain
by Amazon